SO YOU WANNA BE A ~~DRONE PILOT~~? REMOTE PILOT IN COMMAND

SO YOU WANNA BE A ~~DRONE PILOT~~? REMOTE PILOT IN COMMAND

PERK PERKINS

ASPERGILL PRESS
www.aspergillpress.com

Copyright © 2016 By Perk Perkins

All rights reserved. No part of this publication may be reproduced, distributed, or transmitted without the prior written permission of the publisher.

Aspergill Press
www.aspergillpress.com

Cover and Layout by Aspergill Press

All artwork, pictures and text used with permission.

Printed in the United States of America

ISBN 978-0-9856946-4-7

Second Edition
10 9 8 7 6 5 4 3 2 1

Table of Contents

PREFACE	VII
1. PART 107	1
2. AIRSPACE CLASSIFICATION, OPERATING REQUIREMENTS AND FLIGHT RESTRICTIONS	19
3A. AVIATION WEATHER SOURCES	59
3B. EFFECTS OF WEATHER	65
4. SMALL UNMANNED AIRCRAFT LOADING	73
5. EMERGENCY PROCEDURES	77
6. CREW RESOURCE MANAGEMENT (CRM)	81
7. RADIO COMMUNICATION PROCEDURES	83
8. DETERMINING THE PERFORMANCE OF SMALL UNMANNED AIRCRAFT	87

9. PHYSIOLOGICAL FACTORS (INCLUDING DRUGS AND ALCOHOL) AFFECTING PILOT PERFORMANCE   **89**

10. AERONAUTICAL DECISION-MAKING (ADM) AND JUDGMENT   **95**

11. AIRPORT OPERATIONS   **103**

12. MAINTENANCE AND PREFLIGHT INSPECTION PROCEDURES   **111**

APPENDIX 1 STEP-BY-STEP TO GET YOUR LICENSE   **117**

APPENDIX 2 ABBREVIATIONS   **119**

SAMPLE UAS EXAM   **123**

PREFACE

The FAA has chosen an incremental approach to permitting commercial small Unmanned Aircraft System (sUAS) operations. This includes the use of waivers, as long as safety is maintained or increased.

Unlike the "Affordable Care Act", better known as "Obamacare", which was mysteriously written behind close doors (and was passed by Congress before it was read), the FAA requested and received over 4,600 comments on how the new drone law should be structured. Comments were submitted by everyone from large corporations, such as Google and Amazon, down to local organizations including the Nez Perce Tribe and the Wisconsin Society of Land Surveyors.

I read these 4,600 comments, so you don't have to. The adoption of the incremental approach had its champions, such as pilots, and its detractors, such as Amazon. Here is a tiny sample of the convoluted language you need to deal with to read the preamble:

"...the commenters asserted that by delaying the integration of certain operations, such as beyond-visual-line-of-sight operations, until a future rulemaking, the FAA would also delay the benefits associated with those operations until the pertinent future rulemaking is complete."
Do you think you could stay awake through 624 single-spaced pages of that?

"Not so bad," you say? Check out what the FAA sounds like when they want to explain why they chose Sec 333 and not Sec 332:

"Because the statutory text of section 332(b)(1) applies only to those UAS that do not meet the requirements of section 333, sections 332 and 333 cannot both apply to the same UAS. The Department is pursuing this rulemaking under section 333 because section 333(b)(2) allows it to find that airworthiness certification is not necessary for small UAS that will be subject to this rule. As discussed in section III.J.3 of this preamble, the Department has indeed found that mandatory airworthiness certification is unnecessary to ensure the safety or security of these types of small UAS operations. However, unlike section 333(b)(2), section 332 does not contain a provision that would allow the Department to find that airworthiness certification should not be required for a small UAS. Because airworthiness certification is normally a statutory requirement imposed by 49 U.S.C. 44704 and 44711(a)(1), the FAA would have to include an airworthiness certification requirement in this rule if it were to conduct this rulemaking under section 332 rather than section 333."

That's a good thing, right? Yes, airworthiness certification is not required. The entire regulation is posted on the FAA website for your enjoyment.

"After considering the comments, the FAA has decided to proceed incrementally and issue a final rule that immediately integrates the lowest-risk small UAS operations into the NAS. As some commenters pointed out, delaying the integration of the lowest-risk small UAS operations until issues associated with higher-risk operations have been addressed would needlessly delay the realization of societal benefits associated with integrating UAS operations for which the pertinent safety issues have been addressed. In addition, the immediate integration of the lowest-risk small UAS operations into the NAS would provide the FAA with additional operational experience and data that could be used to assist with the integration of higher-risk operations." This new rule, Part 107, is why we can fly small Unmanned Aircraft (sUA) now, before ALL the rules have been finalized and the technology tested.

The goal of the FAA is safety.

If you provide false or altered reports or records you will be subject to punishment by the FAA.

There are twelve topics you need to know to achieve your Remote Pilot Certificate with Small Unmanned Aircraft Systems Rating:

1. CFR 14, Part 107 - New regulations relating to sUAS, limitations and flight operation;
2. Airspace classification, operating requirements and flight restrictions affecting sUA operation;
3. Aviation weather sources and effects of weather on sUA performance;
4. sUA loading;
5. Emergency procedures;
6. Crew resource management;
7. Radio communication procedures;
8. Determining the performance of sUA;
9. Physiological effects, including drugs and alcohol;
10. Aeronautical decision-making and judgment;
11. Airport operations;
12. Maintenance and preflight inspection procedures.

The Test
The Unmanned Aircraft General (UAG) test consists of 60 questions, you must answer at least 70% correct (42 questions) and you have two hours to complete the test. The test is administered at FAA authorized sites on a computer and is multiple choice with three answers. There are 3-5 extra questions mixed in the test that do not count. You just don't know which ones they are, but they are not questions 61-63. So if you've never heard of the question, don't freak out. Make an educated guess or mark for review and come back later.

The FAA provides free sources for this information on their website **www.faa.gov**. In addition to 14 CFR Part 107, the Aeronautical Information Manual (AIM) contains required information and AC 107-2, is also a good sUA specific reference tool. These, the Remote Pilot Study Guide, the Pilot's Handbook and a couple of Safety Alerts for Operators (SAFO) are combined, collated and condensed into this book.

I recommend you read "The Remote Pilot Study Guide" online one time. It goes into more detail about weather and aeronautical decision making, but totally ignores other areas. You may not pass the exam if you only study the FAA's "Remote Pilot Study Guide."

I tried to walk a thin line between providing too much information and not enough. There is no point in putting a star next to testable material, because everything in Chapters One through Twelve is testable. The FAA has more than 60 test topics, so every test won't see every topic. I actually had the same question twice on my exam, but they used different examples.

Safe flying,

Perk

1. PART 107

Intro
THE PURPOSE OF PART 107 IS UAS SAFETY!

OPERATIONAL LIMITATIONS

•Small Unmanned Aircraft (sUA) must weigh less than 55 lbs. This includes all cargo, fuel, gear, etc.

•Visual line-of-sight (VLOS) only; the sUA must remain within VLOS of the Remote Pilot In Control (RPIC) and the person manipulating the flight controls (when used) and within VLOS of the visual observer (VO) (when used). Waivable.

•The sUA must remain close enough to the RPIC, the person manipulating the flight controls and the VO to be able to see the sUA with unaided vision. Corrective lenses (glasses/contacts) may be worn. The FAA expects you to see 20/20 and have normal field of view. Binoculars are OK for situational awareness.

•sUA may not operate over any persons not directly participating in the operation or who are not under a covered structure or not inside a covered stationary vehicle. You cannot fly over innocent people. Waivable.

•Daylight operations only. Dawn (30 minutes before official sunrise) and dusk (30 minutes after official sunset local time) (together called twilight) flying is permitted with proper anti-collision lighting visible 3 statute miles. Night flying is prohibited, but waivable. Night is defined as the time between dusk and dawn (or in Alaska, during the period a prominent unlighted object cannot be seen from a distance of 3 statute miles or the sun is more than 6 degrees below the horizon.)

•Must yield right of way to all other aircraft. Yielding the right of way means that the small unmanned aircraft must give way to the other aircraft or vehicle and may not pass over, under or ahead of the other aircraft/vehicle unless well clear. Well clear means that the small unmanned aircraft is far enough away from the other aircraft or vehicle that it no longer presents a hazard to that aircraft or vehicle. This includes during emergency avoidance action. When two sUAs approach each other, each RPIC will have to take whatever maneuvers are necessary to ensure that his or her sUA is not flying so close to other UA as to create a collision hazard. This is waivable.

•May use Visual Observer (VO), but not required. A VO is a person who assists the RPIC and the person manipulating the flight controls (if used) to see and avoid other air traffic or objects aloft or on the ground. The VO is an optional crew member not required to obtain an airman certificate and will be positioned by the RPIC to best do their job. The crew can use radios or other technology to maintain required communications as determined by the RPIC. Waivable.

The VO, the RPIC and the person manipulating the flight controls of the sUAS (if that person is not the RPIC) will be required to coordinate and communicate in order to:
(1) Scan the airspace where the small unmanned aircraft is operating for any potential collision hazard.
(2) Maintain 100 % awareness of the position of the sUA through direct visual observation, this includes attitude, location, altitude and direction of flight.
(3) Determine the sUA poses a threat to life or property.

- First-person view camera cannot satisfy "see-and-avoid" requirement, but can be used as long as requirement is satisfied in other ways. To ensure the RPIC can safely see-and-avoid other aircraft and people and property on the ground, the sUA:

1 May only be operated within visual line of sight. (Waivable.)
2 Must yield right of way to all other aircraft.
3 May only be operated between the hours of sunrise and sunset. (Waivable.)
4 Must meet minimum weather and visibility requirements.

- Autonomous flight is permitted but the RPIC must be able to take immediate control to divert the sUA to avoid collision or hazards. Autonomous flight is the same as having an unlicensed person flying the sUA. The RPIC is still in command and all rules must still be followed, such as Visual Line Of Sight (VLOS) and only one sUA under command.

- Minimum weather visibility of 3 miles, measured from control station. Flight visibility is defined as the average slant distance from the control station at which prominent unlighted objects may be seen and identified by day and prominent lighted objects may be seen and identified by night. Minimum distance from clouds is 500 feet below and 2,000 feet horizontally away from the cloud. Waivable.

- Maximum ground speed of 100 mph (87 knots). Waivable.

- Maximum altitude of 400 feet above ground level (AGL) or remain within a 400 foot radius of a structure and within 400 feet of its top. Operating ceiling limit is waivable.

- Operations in Class B, C, D and E airspace are allowed with the required ATC permission. In order to avoid interfering with operations in a traffic pattern, remote pilots should avoid operating in the traffic pattern or published approach corridors used by manned aircraft at any airport, heliport, or seaplane base. The RPIC should operate the sUA in such a way that the manned-aircraft pilot need not alter their flight path in the traffic pattern or on a published instrument approach, to avoid a potential collision with you. You must be able to define these airspaces. Waivable.

• Operations in Class G airspace are allowed without ATC permission.

• No operation of sUAs in airspace restricted by NOTAMs, unless authorized by ATC or a Certificate Of Waiver or Authorization.

• No person may act as RPIC or VO for more than one sUA operation at one time. Waivable.

• No operations from a moving aircraft. Waivable.

• No operations from a moving vehicle (land or water) unless the operation is over a sparsely populated area. Waivable.

• No careless or reckless operations which would endanger the life or property of another. The FAA has issued guidance (FAA Order 8900.1, vol. 14, ch. 3, sec. 5), which summarizes the pertinent case law, and provides examples of conduct considered careless or reckless. In the words of the FAA, "For example, failure to consider weather conditions near structures, trees, or rolling terrain when operating in a densely populated area could be determined as careless or reckless operation." The FAA also states that you cannot drive a car and fly your sUA safely. (Hint: This impertinent behavior is often preceded by the imperative statement, "Hey, watch this!")

• No carriage of hazardous materials.

• Requires preflight inspection and briefing for people who are directly participating in the sUA operation by the RPIC.

PART 107

Prior to flight, assess the operating environment and consider risks to persons and property in the vicinity, both on the surface and in the air, to ensure that the sUA will pose no hazard to other aircraft, people, or property in the event of a loss of control. And inform the crew about the operating conditions, emergency procedures, contingency procedures, roles, responsibilities, weather conditions, airspace restrictions, ground location of crew and potential hazards.

•A person may not operate a small unmanned aircraft if he or she knows or has reason to know of any physical or mental condition that would interfere with the safe operation of a sUAS. Paragraph107.17 requires the RPIC to abstain from sUA operations if they know or have reason to know that they have a physical or mental condition that would interfere with the safe operation of the flight. Part 107 does not include a list of disqualifying medical conditions. A person with bipolar disorder would violate § 107.17 only if their bipolar disorder interfered with the safe operation of a sUAS. The FAA emphasizes that those with a medical history or who are experiencing medical symptoms that would prevent them from safely participating in a sUA operation or that raises a reasonable concern, cannot claim to have no known medical conditions.

•Foreign owned and operated sUAs are allowed to operate under part 107 if they satisfy the requirements of 14 CFR Part 375.41, which requires a Foreign Aircraft Permit. This includes US-registered sUAs owned by non-citizen/non-permanent residents. You can read every regulation at **www.ecfr.gov**. Select "Title 14 - Aeronautics and Space" and then click on "Browse parts column" "200-399" to read 375.

•External load operations are allowed if the object being carried by the sUA is securely attached and does not adversely affect the flight characteristics or controllability of the aircraft. Flight characteristics mean the stability of the sUA, while controllability refers to the maneuverability of the sUA. To satisfy these requirements, the RPIC must examine the equipment used for lifting or securing the payload to ensure that it is in good condition, strong enough for the task and attached in a manner so there is no unintended shifting or detaching of the payload.

•Transportation of property for compensation or hire is allowed, but these restrictions are not waivable:
The aircraft, including its attached systems, payload and cargo must weigh less than 55 pounds total, the sUA is operated in Visual-line-of-sight and NOT from a moving vehicle, you can determine the sUA's location, altitude, attitude and direction, yield the right-of-way, maintain see-and-avoid, never carry "hazardous materials" and are a US citizen or permanent resident.

You can drop an object as long as it does not cause a hazard to aircraft or people or things on the ground and the flight occurs wholly within the bounds of a State and does not involve transport between (1) Hawaii and another place in Hawaii through airspace outside Hawaii; (2) the District of Columbia and another place in the District of Columbia; or (3) a territory or possession of the United States and another place in the same territory or possession.

•When defining an air carrier performing air transport, the Department looks for:
1. How the transportation is being marketed and offered to customers.
2. Whether the transporting entity has existing aviation economic authority.
3. Extent to which the people or goods are being transported as part of an inter- or multi- state network.

•Public operations conducted in accordance with a COA (Certificate Of Authority), will not be affected by the requirements of Part 107.

PART 107

<u>Waivers</u>
• Many of the Part 107 restrictions are waivable if the applicant demonstrates that their <u>operation can be conducted safely</u> under the terms of the Certificate of Waiver (CoW). Apply for your CoW at www.faa.gov/uas/request_waiver. Allow at least 90 days for approval. You must keep your CoW with you when you are flying. The following are waivable:
1. Operation from a moving vehicle or aircraft. (Does not include transport for compensation or hire.)
2. Daylight operations.
3. Visual-line-of-sight
4. Visual Observer
5. Operating multiple aircraft systems
6. Yielding right-of-way
7. Operation over people
8. Operation in certain airspace
9. Operating limitations for sUA (speed, size, altitude, etc.)

RPIC CERTIFICATION AND RESPONSIBILITIES

• Part 107 establishes a Remote Pilot In Command (RPIC) position who:
1. Must be designated before or during flight, but can change inflight to another licensed RPIC. To finalize the switch the new commander must make an affirmative statement such as, "I have command."
2. Will have final authority and responsibility for the operation and safety of a sUA operation conducted under Part 107.
3. The RPIC will be required to obtain a remote pilot certificate with a sUA rating. This certificate must be accessible while flying.
4. An uncertificated person is permitted to manipulate the flight controls of the sUAS as long as they are directly supervised by a RPIC.
    4.1. The RPIC must have the ability to immediately take direct control of the small unmanned aircraft.
    4.2. Throughout the entire flight of the sUA, the RPIC and the person manipulating the flight controls of the

sUAS must both have the ability to see the sUA, unaided by any device, other than corrective lenses.
5. Must ensure that all persons directly participating in the sUA operation, including the visual observer, are informed about the operating conditions, emergency procedures, contingency procedures, roles and responsibilities and potential hazards.
6. In case of an in-flight emergency, the RPIC will be permitted to deviate from any rule in Part 107, as necessary, to deal with the emergency. An RPIC who exercises this emergency power to deviate from the rules of Part 107 will be required, upon FAA request, to send a written report to the FAA explaining the deviation.
7. Is responsible for ensuring that the sUA operation complies with all applicable FAA regulations.
8. Must ensure that the sUA will not pose an undue hazard to other aircraft, people, or property on the ground if positive control is lost.
9. Is in charge of only one airborne aircraft at a time.
10. Will, upon request, make their remote pilot certificate available to the FAA Administrator.

•A person operating a sUAS must either hold a remote pilot airman certificate with a sUA rating or be under the direct supervision of a person who holds a remote pilot certificate.

•To qualify for a remote pilot certificate, a person must:

Demonstrate aeronautical knowledge by either:

Passing an initial aeronautical knowledge test at an FAA-approved knowledge testing center; or
Hold a part 61 pilot certificate, complete a flight review within the previous 24 months and complete a sUAS online training course provided by the FAA.

Be vetted by the Transportation Security Administration.

Be at least 16 years old.

PART 107

Be able to read, write, speak and understand English. Waivable for medical reasons.

Not have any physical or medical conditions that would interfere with operating a sUAS.

- Part 61 pilot certificate holders can obtain a temporary remote pilot certificate immediately upon submission of their application for a permanent certificate.

- Until international standards are developed, foreign-certificated UA pilots will be required to obtain a US issued remote pilot certificate with a small UAS rating to operate in the US.

- Aeronautical Knowledge Recency
No one may serve as RPIC if they have not passed an aeronautical knowledge exam within the past 24 months. This could be the initial test, the recurrent test or the Part 61 test.

An RPIC must:

- Make available to the FAA, upon request, the sUAS for inspection or testing and all documents/records required to be kept under the rule.

- Report to the FAA within 10 days of any operation that results in serious or fatal injury, loss of consciousness or property damage of at least $500 (repair or replace whichever is less).

A serious injury is ranked 3 or higher on the Abbreviated Injury Scale (AIS). The FAA example is: "a "serious injury" is if a person requires hospitalization, but the injury is fully reversible (including, but not limited to, head trauma, broken bone(s), or laceration(s) to the skin that requires suturing)."

The $500 repair/replace damage does not count your sUA. The FAA example: "a small UA damages a property whose fair market value is $200, and it would cost $600 to repair the damage. Because the fair market value is below $500, this accident is not required to be reported. Similarly, if the aircraft causes $200 worth of damage to property whose fair market value is $600, that accident is also not required to be reported because the repair cost is below $500."

You can report your accident by phone to the FAA Regional Operations Center (ROC) or online at **www.faa.gov/uas/**. The report should include:
1. sUAS RPIC's name and contact info;
2. sUAS RPIC's FAA airman certificate number;
3. sUAS registration number issued to the aircraft, (FAA registration number);
4. Location of the accident;
5. Date of the accident;
6. Time of the accident;
7. Person(s) injured and extent of injury, if any or known;
8. Property damaged and extent of damage, if any or known; and
9. Description of what happened.

State where accident occurred - FAA Regional Operations Center phone number:
DC, DE, MD, NJ, NY, PA, WV, and VA - 404-305-5150
AL, CT, FL, GA, KY, MA, ME, MS, NC, NH, PR, RI, SC, TN, VI, and VT - 404-305-5156
AK, AS, AZ, CA, CO, GU, HI, ID, MP, MT, NV, OR, UT, WA, and WY - 425-227-1999
AR, IA, IL, IN, KS, LA, MI, MN, MO, ND, NE, NM, OH, OK, SD, TX, and WI - 817-222-5006

Some accidents need to be reported to the National Transportation Safety Board (NTSB). Check their website at: www.ntsb.gov

•Conduct a preflight inspection, to include specific aircraft and control station systems checks, to ensure the sUAS is in a condition for safe operation. Complete info on this inspection is in Chapter 12 Maintenance and Inspections.

PART 107

•A RPIC may deviate from the provisions of Part 107 to the extent necessary, in response to an in-flight emergency. Because Part 107 will allow a deviation only during an in-flight emergency, this deviation cannot be taken for situations that were expected or foreseen prior to the takeoff of the sUA. The FAA also emphasizes that the RPIC must always prioritize the safety of human life above all other considerations. This means one drop of human blood is worth more than the entire sUAS. The RPIC must, upon FAA request, submit a report to the FAA if they have exercised their emergency powers. RPICs must be proficient in emergency procedures and the proper exercise of emergency authority.

AIRCRAFT REQUIREMENTS

All sUA must be registered. Commercial registration is $5 per aircraft. Hobby registration is $5 per hobbyist, for unlimited aircraft.

•Registration
Your sUA will comply with the existing registration requirements specified in § 91.203(a)(2) when you follow paragraphs listed under 14 CFR part 48, Registration and Marking Requirements for Small Unmanned Aircraft, summarized here. You must keep your registration with you when you are flying to present to authorities. You can register your sUA online at:
www.faa.gov/uas/registration/. You don't have to register your sUA, if on takeoff, it weighs less than 0.55 pounds. You should cancel your registration if the sUA is sold, lost or transferred. Failure to register can result in civil fines up to $27,500 and criminal fines up to $250,000 and/or three years in prison.

Requirement to register
The sUA must be registered and properly marked by its owner. The "owner" can be a US Citizen, a permanent

resident or a US corporation and must use their legal name. Humans must be at least 13 years of age and fill out the online form at the FAA sUA site. ("Owner" includes a buyer in possession, a bailee, a lessee of a sUA under a contract of conditional sale and the assignee of that person. Registration does not prove ownership.)

For all commercial use
The information required includes: name, address, email, aircraft manufacturer and model name, aircraft serial number and any other info required by the Administrator.

For use a model aircraft only
The information required includes: name, address, email and any other info required by the Administrator.

Registration marking
The FAA will issue a Certificate of Aircraft Registration and a unique identifier (ID) number upon successful completion of the application. The ID number must be legible and fixed to the aircraft during the entire flight. The ID must readily accessible and visible and can be in a compartment which can be opened without tools, like the battery compartment on some sUA.

For questions about registration email **UASregistration@faa.gov** or call (877) 396-4636, 10am to 6 pm ET, Monday through Friday.

•FAA airworthiness certification is not required. However, the RPIC must conduct a preflight check of the sUAS to ensure that it is in a condition for safe operation.

MODEL AIRCRAFT

•The rule codifies the FAA's enforcement authority in Part 101 by prohibiting model aircraft operators from endangering the safety of the NAS.

•Part 107 considers your sUA a model aircraft if it satisfies all of the criteria specified:

PART 107

1. It must be capable of sustained flight.
2. It must be flow within visual line of sight.
3. It must be flown for hobby or recreational purposes (not for compensation).
4. It is flown in accordance with community-based set of safety guidelines, within a <u>nationwide community-based organization</u>. (This "nationwide" phrase was added on purpose, don't blow it off.)
5. The aircraft is limited to 55 pounds.
6. The aircraft does not interfere and gives way to other air traffic.
7. When flown within 5 miles of an airport, the operator of the aircraft provides the airport operator and the airport air traffic control tower (when an air traffic facility is located at the airport) with prior notice of the operation.

•Part 107 does not apply to:
 1. model aircraft
 2. air carrier operations;
 3. international operations;
 4. public aircraft operations;
 5. moored balloons,
 6. kites
 7. amateur rockets
 8. unmanned free balloons.

Grandfathering of Section 333 Exemption Holders
•The FAA allows Section 333 exemption holders to continue operating under the terms and conditions of their exemption until its expiration or fly under Part 107, as long as the operation falls under Part 107.

PART 107 SUMMARY

Operational Limitations

• Unmanned aircraft must weigh less than 55 lbs.

• Visual line-of-sight (VLOS) only; the sUA must remain within VLOS of the RPIC and the person manipulating the flight controls (when used) and within VLOS of the visual observer (when used).

• At all times the small unmanned aircraft must remain close enough to the RPIC and the person manipulating the flight controls of the sUAS for those people to be capable of seeing the aircraft with vision unaided by any device other than corrective lenses.

• sUA may not operate over any persons not directly participating in the operation or who are not under a covered structure or not inside a covered stationary vehicle.

• Daylight only flying or civil twilight flying (30 minutes before official sunrise to 30 minutes after official sunset, local time) allowable with proper lighting.

• Must yield right of way to all other aircraft.

• May use visual observer (VO) but not required.

• First-person view camera cannot satisfy "see-and-avoid" requirement but can be used as long as requirement is satisfied in other ways.

• Maximum ground speed of 100 mph (87 knots).

• Maximum altitude of 400 feet above ground level (AGL) or, if higher than 400 feet AGL, remain within 400 feet of a structure.

• Minimum weather visibility of 3 miles, measured from

PART 107

control station.

•Operations in Class B, C, D and E airspace are allowed with the required ATC permission.

•Operations in Class G airspace are allowed without ATC permission.

•No person may act as a RPIC or VO for more than one unmanned aircraft operation at one time.

•No operations from a moving aircraft.

•No operations from a moving vehicle unless the operation is over a sparsely populated area.

•No careless or reckless operations.

•No carriage of hazardous materials.

•Requires preflight inspection by the RPIC.

•A person may not operate a small unmanned aircraft if he or she knows or has reason to know of any physical or mental condition that would interfere with the safe operation of a sUAS.

•Foreign-registered small unmanned aircraft are allowed to operate under part 107 if they satisfy the requirements of part 375.

•External load operations are allowed if the object being carried by the unmanned aircraft is securely attached and does not adversely affect the flight characteristics or controllability of the aircraft.

•Transportation of property for compensation or hire allowed provided that-

> •The aircraft, including its attached systems, payload and cargo weigh less than 55 pounds

total;

•The flight is conducted within visual line of sight and not from a moving vehicle or aircraft; and

•The flight occurs wholly within the bounds of a State and does not involve transport between (1) Hawaii and another place in Hawaii through airspace outside Hawaii; (2) the District of Columbia and another place in the District of Columbia; or (3) a territory or possession of the United States and another place in the same territory or possession.

•Most of the above restrictions are waivable if the applicant demonstrates that his or her operation can safely be conducted under the terms of the Certificate Of Waiver.

RPIC Certification and Responsibilities
•Establishes a RPIC position.

•A person operating a sUAS must either hold a remote pilot airman certificate with a sUA rating or be under the direct supervision of a person who does hold a remote pilot certificate (RPIC).

•To qualify for a remote pilot certificate, a person must:

Demonstrate aeronautical knowledge by either:
Passing an initial aeronautical knowledge test at an FAA-approved knowledge testing center; or
Hold a part 61 pilot certificate, complete a flight review within the previous 24 months and complete a small UAS online training course provided by the FAA.

Be vetted by the Transportation Security Administration.

Be at least 16 years old.

PART 107 SUMMARY

•Part 61 pilot certificate holders can obtain a temporary remote pilot certificate immediately upon submission of their application for a permanent certificate.

•Until international standards are developed, foreign-certificated UAS pilots will be required to obtain a remote pilot certificate with a sUA rating.

A RPIC must:

•Make available to the FAA, upon request, the sUAS for inspection or testing, and any associated documents/records required to be kept under the rule.

•Report to the FAA within 10 days of any operation that results in serious or fatal injury, loss of consciousness or property damage of at least $500.

•Conduct a preflight inspection, to include specific aircraft and control station systems checks, to ensure the sUAS is in a condition for safe operation.

•Ensure that the sUA complies with the existing registration requirements specified in § 91.203(a)(2).

•A RPIC may deviate from the requirements of this rule in response to an in-flight emergency.

Aircraft Requirements
•FAA airworthiness certification is not required. However, the RPIC must conduct a preflight check of the sUA to ensure that it is in a condition for safe operation.

Model Aircraft
•Part 107 does not apply to model aircraft that satisfy all of the criteria specified in section 336 of Public Law 112-95.
•The rule codifies the FAA's enforcement authority in part 101 by prohibiting model aircraft operators from endangering the safety of the NAS.

Airspace Definitions

FL 600

Class A

18,000' MSL

Class B

Class C

Class D

Class E

Class G

1,200' AGL
700' AGL

Nontowered airport with instrument approach

Nontowered airport with no instrument approach

14,500' MSL

2. Airspace Classification, Operating
Requirements and Flight Restrictions

Intro
Airspace is broken down into two categories: regulatory and nonregulatory. These two categories are divided into four types of airspace: controlled, uncontrolled, special use and other. The more air traffic, the tighter the control.

Controlled Airspace
The "controlled" means that an airport tower is performing the air traffic control (ATC). You can request permission to fly you sUA in controlled airspace at the link on www.faa.gov/uas/

Class A airspace starts at 18,000 feet mean sea level (MSL) and extends up to 60,000 feet (FL600). You can't fly your drone here legally, but you still need to be able to define it for the test.

Class B surrounds the busiest airports from the ground to 10,000 feet above MSL. It is tiered with the tiers getting larger higher up. It looks like an upside down wedding cake with two or more tiers. You must receive authorization from the ATC before flying here.

Class C is like Class B, but at smaller airports. Class C extends up to 4,000 feet above airport's elevation MSL. It has one tier. You need ATC permission to fly here.

Class D is for small airports and extends up to 2,500 feet above airport's elevation MSL. It looks like a cylinder. You must have permission from ATC to fly here.

Class E airspace is a "catch-all" for all other controlled airspace not designated Class A, B, C or D. Class E airspace is used to travel around the country (such as Federal Flyways) and can be from the ground (usually 1,200 feet above ground level (AGL)) up to an elevation of 18,000 MSL (the bottom of Class A airspace) and from above the top of Class A airspace at FL600 (60,000 MSL) up. Class E airspace is shown on Sectional Charts (Sectionals). You do not usually need ATC permission to fly in Class E airspace, unless it is near an airport.

Two methods exist for the RPIC to get authorization for sUA operations in Class B, C, D, and the lateral boundaries of the surface area of Class E airspace designated for an airport are:
1. Seek approval from the ATC facility with jurisdiction over the airspace where you want to fly.
2. Request an FAA waiver from this provision to fly in Class B through E airspace on the website.

Uncontrolled Airspace
"Uncontrolled" does not mean you can do what you want, it means a tower is not currently controlling this area. Class G airspace is the "catch-all" for ALL uncontrolled airspace. By definition it is not Class A, B, C, D or E. It extends from the surface to the bottom of Class E. This is where you want to fly your sUA. There are small airports in Class G space, with no operating tower. Be aware of them.

Special Use Airspace/ Special Area of Operation (SAO)
This is airspace where certain activities must be confined

AIRSPACE CLASSIFICATION, OPERATING REQUIREMENTS
AND FLIGHT RESTRICTIONS

or non-participating aircraft are limited in operations. "Special Use Airspace can create limitations on the mixed use of airspace." The Special Use Airspace shown on instrument charts includes area name or number, effective altitude, time and weather conditions of operation, controlling agency and chart panel location.

Prohibited Areas – ("P" followed by number, P-40) Defined dimensions where aircraft cannot fly for security or other national welfare reasons which are published in Federal Register and shown on charts. This includes places like the National Mall in Washington D.C., which is surrounded by the White House and congressional buildings. You can always ask permission or get a waiver if you need to fly here for some reason.

Restricted Areas – ("R" followed by a number (R-4401)) <u>Sometimes</u> you can fly here, but it is hazardous to do so without authorization. Think of artillery ranges and guided missile launches. They might look OK, until you have a guided missile chasing your sUA. When the restricted area is not active and control has been returned to ATC, you can request permission to fly in this area. Restricted area information can be found on the back of the chart.

SO YOU WANNA BE A DRONE PILOT?

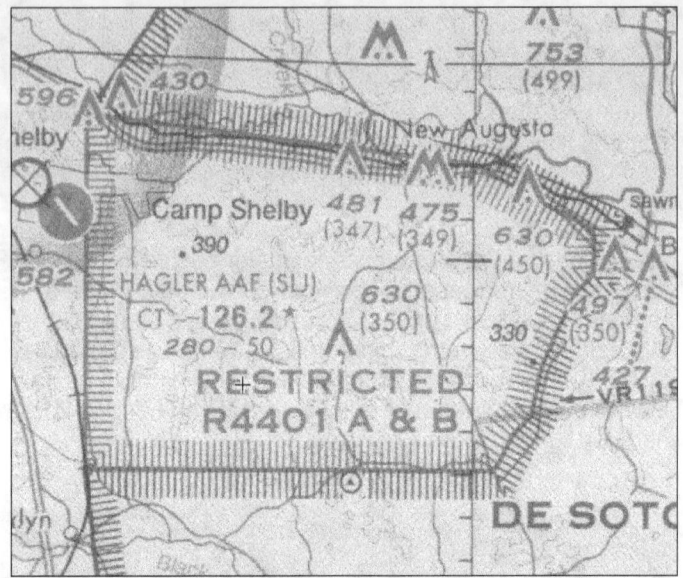

Warning Areas ("W" followed by a number (W-237)) Similar to restricted area except Warning Areas extend 3 nautical miles (NM) from the coast, are hazardous to non-participating aircraft and not necessarily under sole US control. The Warning Area may cover domestic water, international water or both.

Military Operation Areas (MOAs) (named, such as "Camden Ridge MOA") Vertical and lateral airspace limits separate IFR traffic from military training. ATC can clear traffic through when MOA is in use, if possible, or rerouting may be required. MOAs are shown on Sectionals, VFR terminal area and en route low altitude charts. Complete MOA info, like controlling agency and times and dates, are on the back of Sectionals.

AIRSPACE CLASSIFICATION, OPERATING REQUIREMENTS
AND FLIGHT RESTRICTIONS

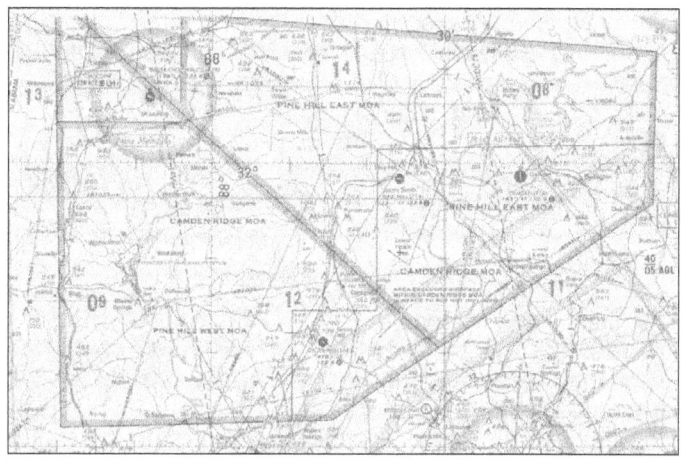

Alert Areas ("A" followed by number (A-211)) Area of high traffic of pilot training or unusual aerial activity requiring increased alertness. You can fly here, but be extra-super careful about other things in the air.

Controlled Firing Areas (CFAs) These are not shown on charts. You, the pilot don't do anything. The hazardous activity stops when the spotter, radar or lookout sees your aircraft approaching. Because the pilot does not do anything, THESE ARE NOT SHOWN ON CHARTS!

Other Airspace Areas

Local Airport Advisory (LAA) Airport information from Flight Services includes advisories, automated weather with voice broadcasting, a continuous Automated Surface Observing System (ASOS)/Automated Weather Observing Station (AWOS) data display and other manual observation and instrument readings available to the specialist.

Military Training Routes (MTRs)(IR or VR followed by four numbers when no segment above 1,500 feet AGL (IR1206,VR1207) or three numbers when one or more segments is above 1,500 feet AGL (IR206, VR 207)) These are high speed, low altitude practice routes for the military, usually below 10,000 feet MSL to the surface. VFR Sectionals contain military information such as IR, VR, MOA, restricted areas, warning areas and alert areas. (Remember, only CFAs do not appear on charts.)

Military Training Route (MTR)

Temporary Flight Restrictions (TFR)

A NOTAM (Notice to Airmen) is issued by the flight data center (FDC) to designate a TFR. All NOTAMs begin with the phrase "FLIGHT RESTRICTIONS", followed by location, effective time period, area and altitudes affected, reason for restriction, the FAA facility and phone number and any other important info. You NEED to check the

AIRSPACE CLASSIFICATION, OPERATING REQUIREMENTS AND FLIGHT RESTRICTIONS

NOTAMs before every sUA flight as part of preflight planning. Go to tfr.faa.gov to check your area. Save it on your phone and it could save you a trip to court.

TFRs are issued to:
• Protect persons and property in the air or on the surface from an existing or imminent hazard.
• Provide a safe environment for the operation of disaster relief aircraft.
• Prevent an unsafe congestion of sightseeing aircraft above an incident or event, that may generate a high degree of public interest.
• Protect declared national disasters for humanitarian reasons in the State of Hawaii.
• Protect the President, Vice President, or other public figures.
• Provide a safe environment for space agency operations.

FDC NOTAM 4/0811, which states that "...to the extent practicable, pilots are strongly advised to avoid the airspace above, or in proximity to such sites as power plants (nuclear, hydro-electric, or coal), dams, refineries, industrial complexes, military facilities and other similar facilities. Pilots should not circle as to loiter in the vicinity over these types of facilities."

Parachute Jump Aircraft Operations – Shown on Sectionals and published in the Chart Supplement U.S.

Published VFR Routes – Shown on VFR terminal area planning charts and used to navigate through and around complex airspace. Includes VFR flyway, VFR corridor, Class B airspace transition route, etc.

Terminal Radar Service Areas (TRSAs) - Shown on VFR Sectionals and terminal area charts. This is where you can get additional radar services, it is voluntary. This is Class D airspace, you need permission to fly here.

National Security Areas (NSAs) - Have vertical and lateral dimensions where increased security required on ground. Check for TFRs. Pilots are asked to voluntarily avoid these areas.

Air Defense Identification Zones (ADIZ) - Land and water based and need Defense VFR (DVFR) flight plan to operate VFR in this airspace.

Flight Restricted Zones (FRZ) - In vicinity of Capitol and White House.

Air Traffic Control and the National Airspace System
The primary purpose is to prevent collision of aircraft by expediting and organizing the flow of traffic. The more air traffic, the more air traffic control required.

Operating Rules and Pilot/Equipment Requirements –
Safe flight is a pilot's top priority and can be helped with preflight planning, proper Aeronautical Decision-Making (ADM) and risk management. See-and-avoid is required by the FAA.

VISUAL FLIGHT RULES (VFR) TERMS AND SYMBOLS

RPICs must know the following from the FAA Aeronautical Chart User's Guide website on the "VFR Terms" tab:
http://www.faa.gov/air_traffic/flight_info/aeronav/digital_products/aero_guide/

VFR Terms
These terms are for the Sectional charts, which have a scale of 1:500,000 and are named after a major city. You can learn to identify aeronautical, topographical and obstruction symbols by using the legend.

Wells show up as open black circles with labels, tanks appear as solid black circles with labels.

AIRSPACE CLASSIFICATION, OPERATING REQUIREMENTS
AND FLIGHT RESTRICTIONS

Water Features (Hydrography) appear as two shades of blue. Dark Blue for inland water and lakes and light blue for coastal open water and huge lakes, like the Great Lakes and Lake Okeechobee (O-kah-cho-b).

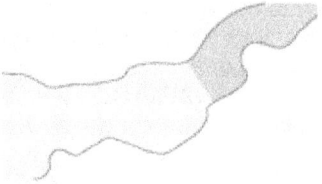

Land Features (Terrain) and Obstructions – The earth's contours and man-made obstructions are shown five ways: contour lines, shaded relief, color tints, obstruction symbols and Maximum Elevation Figures (MEFs).
1. Contour lines join points of same elevation and are spaced at five hundred foot intervals. Intermediate and auxiliary contour lines are spaced closer together to show detail. Widely spaced contour lines means gentle slopes while closely packed contour lines show steep slopes.

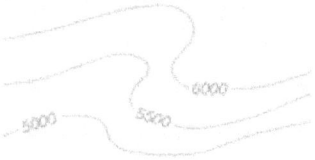

2. Shaded relief shows how terrain appears from the air

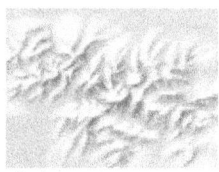

with a northwest light.
3. Color tints show elevation relative to sea level. Lower areas are light green and higher elevations are dark brown.

SO YOU WANNA BE A DRONE PILOT?

4. Obstruction symbols show man-made vertical structures which you could hit. The Aeronautical Information Manual (AIM) has over 1.2 million listed obstructions. "UC" means under construction or the obstruction has not yet been verified. Charts are checked every four years for new or removed obstructions. Sectionals show obstacles over 200 feet Above Ground Level (AGL) (299 feet in yellow city tint) and break them down into under and over 1000 feet. FAA ATC checkpoints use the standard black symbol with max elevation above Mean Sea Level (MSL) in blue. The AGL, if known, will be in parentheses below the MSL.

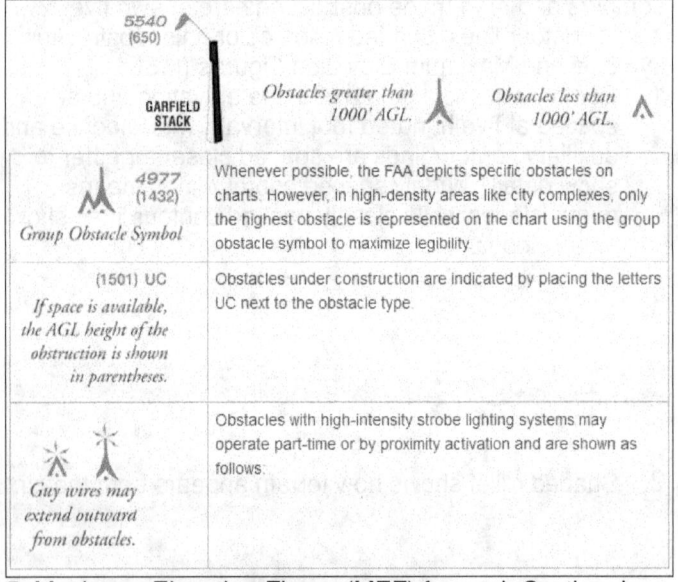

5. Maximum Elevation Figure (MEF) for each Sectional quadrant is shown in blue rounded off to nearest 100 feet MSL. The last two digits are not shown. A Sectional quadrant is bounded by ticked lines every 30 minutes of latitude and longitude. 12,525 feet is shown as 12^6

$$12^5$$

In this example the MEF represents 12,500'.

AIRSPACE CLASSIFICATION, OPERATING REQUIREMENTS
AND FLIGHT RESTRICTIONS

VFR SYMBOLS

The following is condensed from the FAA Aeronautical Chart User's Guide on the FAA website's "VFR SYMBOLS" tab, which is in color:
www.faa.gov/air_traffic/flight_info/aeronav/digital_products/aero_guide/

Airports
Sectional charts break airports down into four categories: hard surface runways greater than 8,069 feet, hard surface runways 1,500-8,069 feet, other than hard-surfaced runways and seaplane bases. Airports are named, show highest runway elevation and runway length. Airports with control towers are shown in blue all others are shown in magenta.

"L" means the lights are on from dusk till dawn. "*L" means to check the Chart Supplement for lighted hours. A blue star means a rotating or flashing airport beacon from dusk till dawn.

"RP18" means the traffic pattern is to the right and to use runway 18. An asterisk (RP*) means you need to check the Chart Supplement, just like for lights.

Public use airports:

 Hard-surfaced runways greater than 8069' or some multiple runways less than 8069'

 Hard-surfaced runways 1500' to 8069'

○ Other than hard-surfaced runways

⚓ Seaplane bases

Military airports:

 Other than hard-surfaced runways

Services available:

 Tick marks around the basic airport symbol indicate that fuel is available and the airport is tended during normal working hours (Monday through Friday 10:00 A.M. to 4:00 P.M. local time).

Other airports with or without services:

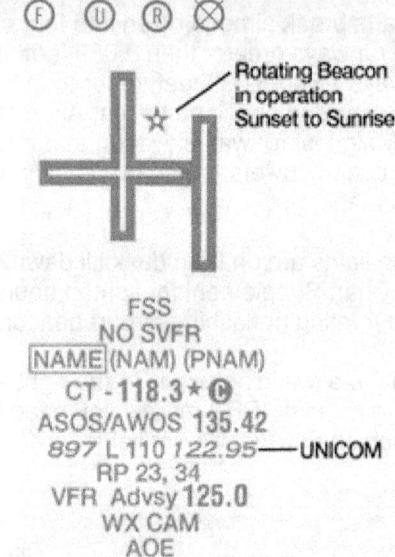

Controlled Airspace Symbols
Class A airspace is not shown on charts, but it is from 18,000 to 60,000 MSL (FL600).
Class B is shown in detail on Sectionals in blue with the ceiling and floor rounded off to hundreds with last two zeros missing.

Class B MSL Altitudes $\frac{90}{20}$

Class C is shown in detail on Sectionals in magenta with the ceiling and floor rounded off to hundreds with last two zeros missing. A magenta box shows distance and radio

AIRSPACE CLASSIFICATION, OPERATING REQUIREMENTS
AND FLIGHT RESTRICTIONS

frequency to be used when entering this airspace.

Class C MSL 70
Altitudes ―
15

T — The figure at left identifies a sector that extends from the surface to the base of the Class B
SFC — Class C Airspace is identified by name BURBANK CLASS C .

Class D is shown as a blue dashed line. When not continuous, the following note in blue, "See NOTAMs/Directory for Class D eff hrs".
Ceilings are shown in blue, rounded to hundreds with last two zeros missing in blue dashed box.

⌈30⌉

Class E Surface (SFC) is shown as a dashed magenta line. When not continuous, the following note in magenta, "See NOTAMs/Directory for Class E (sfc) eff hrs".
Class E is shown as narrow bands of vignette (faded line) marking the lateral and vertical limits. When the floor is 700 feet AGL the vignette is magenta, when it abuts Class G it is blue.

Class E Airspace with floor 700 ft. above surface that laterally abuts Class G Airspace.

Class E Airspace with floor 700 ft. above surface that laterally abuts 1200 ft. or higher Class E Airspace

Class E Airspace with floor 1200 ft. or greater above surface that laterally abuts Class G Airspace

Uncontrolled Airspace
Class G is not designated on charts but it extends up to 14,500 MSL if no other airspace or special use is in force.

Special Use Airspace (SUA)
SUA confines activities and restricts entry to a specific area. SUAs are shown on charts except for Controlled Firing Areas (because you do not change course for CFAs). Prohibited, restricted and warning areas are

labeled in blue and alert and MOAs are labeled in magenta with a letter and number.

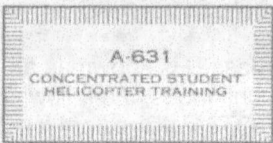

Other Airspace Areas
Mode C Required Airspace extends from the surface up to 10,000 feet MSL with a 30 Nautical Mile (NM) radius of a Class B airport. It is shown as a magenta line with "MODE C" above and distance in NM below.

$$\frac{\text{MODE C}}{\text{30 NM}}$$

National Security Areas are shown as a dashed magenta line

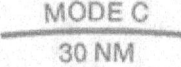

and Special Flight Rules Areas are shown as blue boxes connected by a line on one side.

Both have defined vertical and lateral limits for ground security. Avoid these areas.

Washington D.C. Flight Restricted Zone (FRZ) is shown as closely spaced blue lines connected on one side by a line and encompasses a 13-15 NM radius around the DCA VOR-DME. Special permission is required to fly here.

AIRSPACE CLASSIFICATION, OPERATING REQUIREMENTS
AND FLIGHT RESTRICTIONS

Temporary Flight Restriction (TFR) Areas Relating to National Security are shown as a dashed blue line. This is the only TFR which appears on charts!!

Air Defense Identification Zones (ADIZs) are shown as a line of magenta 8's with a solid line connecting one side. These zones are around Alaska, Canada and US boundaries.

Terminal Radar Service Areas (TRSAs) are shown as a black outline around the area. Ceilings and floors are shown along with the TRSA name.

Military Training Routes (MTRs) are shown as a gray line with black label for VR and IR and an arrow to show direction of flight. They can be between four and sixteen miles wide. (VR206, IR89).

⬅ IR21

Special Military Activity Areas are shown as a black box around the name and radio frequency.

MILITARY TRAINING ROUTES (MTRs)

All IR and VR MTRs are shown, and may extend from the surface upwards. Only the route centerline, direction of flight along the route, and the route designator are depicted - route widths and altitudes are not shown.

Since these routes are subject to change every 56 days, you are cautioned and advised to contact Flight Service for route dimensions and current status for those routes affecting your flight.

Routes with a change in the alignment of the charted route centerline will be indicated in the Aeronautical Chart Bulletin of the Chart Supplement.

DoD users refer to Area Planning AP/1B Military Training Routes North and South America for current routes.

Terminal Area Chart (TAC) Coverage is shown as ¼ inch masked line around the detailed area. The TAC chart shows better detail than a Sectional.

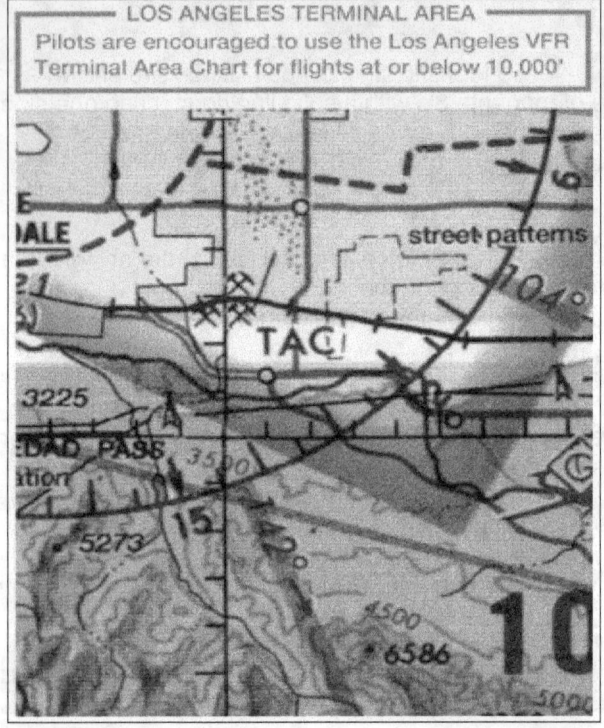

Inset Coverage is shown as 1/8 inch masked line around the area of detail. A blue box contains the title and other important info. See the inset chart for more detail about the area.

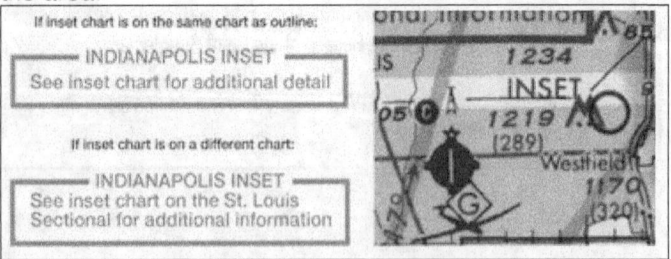

AIRSPACE CLASSIFICATION, OPERATING REQUIREMENTS
AND FLIGHT RESTRICTIONS

Chart Tabulations
Airport Tower communications data is shown in columns. The name, operating hours, primary VHF/UHF Control Tower frequencies, ground control and Automatic Terminal Info Service (ATIS) is listed.

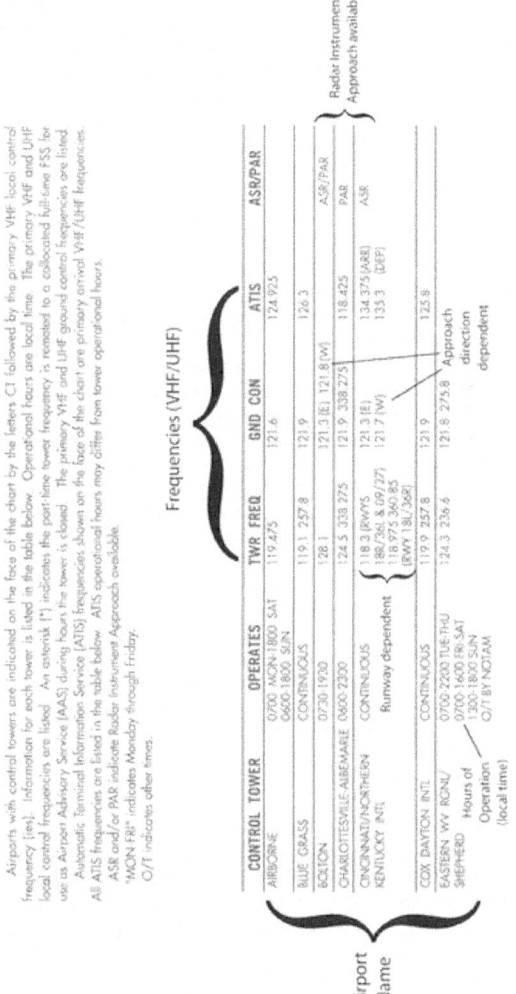

SO YOU WANNA BE A DRONE PILOT?

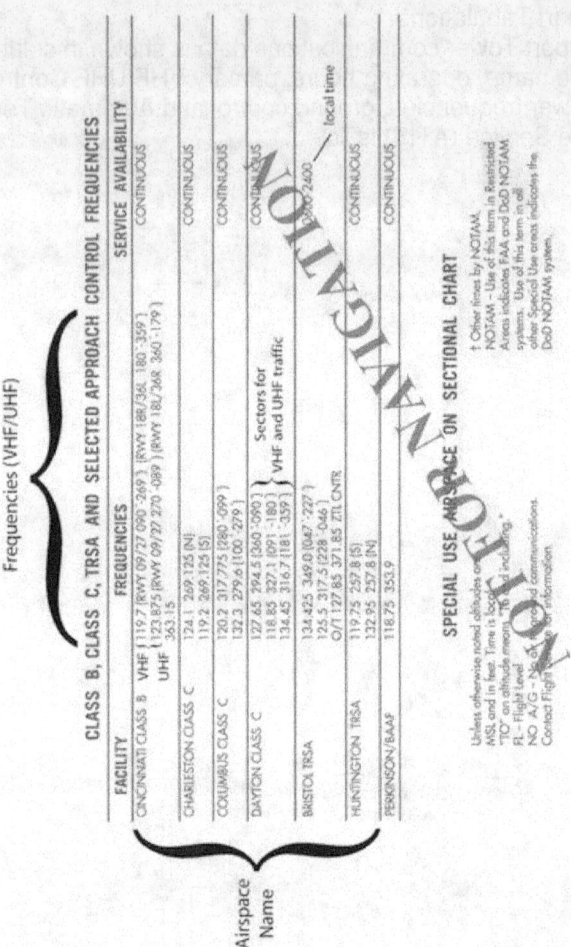

Alert Areas (listed numerically) and Military Operations Areas (MOAs) (listed alphabetically are shown in magenta. Prohibited, Restricted and Warning Areas are shown in blue.
 All include altitude, time of use and controlling agency/contact facility and radio frequency.

AIRSPACE CLASSIFICATION, OPERATING REQUIREMENTS AND FLIGHT RESTRICTIONS

U.S. P—PROHIBITED, R—RESTRICTED, W—WARNING, A—ALERT, MOA—MILITARY OPERATIONS AREA

NUMBER	ALTITUDE	TIME OF USE	CONTROLLING AGENCY/ CONTACT FACILITY	FREQUENCIES —— VHF/UHF
R-6602 A	TO BUT NOT INCL 4000	CONTINUOUS MAY 1-SEP 15 †24 HRS IN ADVANCE	WASHINGTON CNTR	118.75 377.1
R-6602 B	4000 TO BUT NOT INCL 11,000	BY NOTAM 24 HRS IN ADVANCE	WASHINGTON CNTR	118.75 377.1
R-6602 C	11,000 TO BUT NOT INCL 18,000	BY NOTAM 24 HRS IN ADVANCE	WASHINGTON CNTR	118.75 377.1
A 220	TO 4000 AGL	0800-2200	NO A/G	

MOA NAME	ALTITUDE*	TIME OF USE†	CONTROLLING AGENCY/ CONTACT FACILITY	FREQUENCIES —— VHF/UHF
BRUSH CREEK	100 AGL TO BUT NOT INCL 5000	0800-2200 MON-SAT	INDIANAPOLIS CNTR	134.0 135.57
BUCKEYE	5000	0800-2200 MON-FRI 0800-1600 SAT-SUN	INDIANAPOLIS CNTR	134.0 135.57
EVERS	1000 AGL	SR-SS BY NOTAM	WASHINGTON CNTR	

*Altitudes indicate floor of MOA. All MOAs extend to but do not include FL 180 unless otherwise indicated in tabulation or on chart.
†Other times by DoD NOTAM

Sunrise to Sunset

CANADA R—RESTRICTED, D—DANGER AND A—ADVISORY AREA

	NUMBER	LOCATION	ALTITUDE	TIME OF USE	CONTROLLING AGENCY
Restricted	CYR754	CONFEDERATION BRIDGE, PE	TO 500	CONTINUOUS	
Danger	CYD734	HALIFAX, NS	TO FL 200	OCCASIONAL BY NOTAM	MONCTON ACC
Advisory	CYA702 (P)	GREENWOOD, NS	TO 500	CONT DAYLIGHT	
	CYA752 (M)	LIVERPOOL, NS	TO FL 280	CONT DAYLIGHT MON-FRI EXC HOL†	MONCTON ACC

A-Acrobatic   F-Aircraft Test Area   H-Hang Gliding   M-Military Operations   P-Parachuting   S-Soaring   T-Training

SO YOU WANNA BE A DRONE PILOT?

The FAA wants you to know the chart symbols for basic things. These can be found on the FAA Aeronautical Chart User's Guide on the FAA website. Click on the "VFR SYMBOLS" tab to see these in color. You are responsible for the VFR Aeronautical Chart Symbols for Airports, Airspace Information, Navigational and Procedural Information, Chart Limits, Culture, Hydrography and Relief. You DO NOT need to study "Radio Aids to Navigation". See **www.faa.gov/air_traffic/flight_info/aeronav/digital_products/aero_guide/**

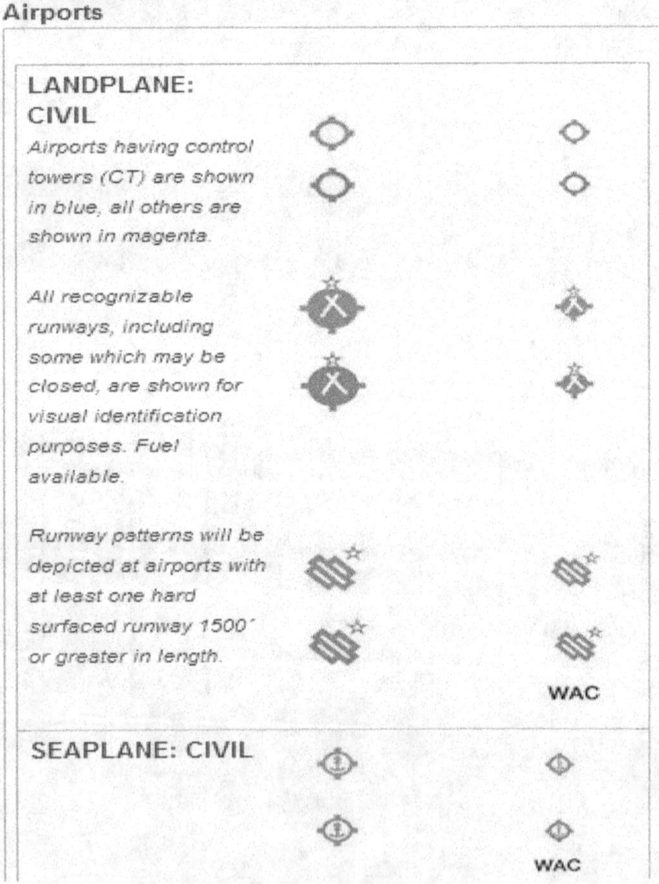

Airports

LANDPLANE: CIVIL

Airports having control towers (CT) are shown in blue, all others are shown in magenta.

All recognizable runways, including some which may be closed, are shown for visual identification purposes. Fuel available.

Runway patterns will be depicted at airports with at least one hard surfaced runway 1500' or greater in length.

WAC

SEAPLANE: CIVIL

WAC

AIRSPACE CLASSIFICATION, OPERATING REQUIREMENTS
AND FLIGHT RESTRICTIONS

LANDPLANE: CIVIL-MILITARY	◉ ◉ ⛌ ⛌	◉ ◉ ⛌ ⛌ WAC
Add appropriate note as required for hard surfaced runways only: "(CLOSED)"	⊗ ABANDONED - Depicted for landmark value or to prevent confusion with an adjacent usable landing area. (Normally at least 3000' paved)	⊗ WAC
SEAPLANE: EMERGENCY *Fuel not available or complete information is not available.*	⚓	⚓ WAC
HELIPORT *(Selected)*	Ⓗ	Ⓗ WAC
ULTRALIGHT FLIGHT PARK *(Selected)*	Ⓕ	Not shown on WAC

SO YOU WANNA BE A DRONE PILOT?

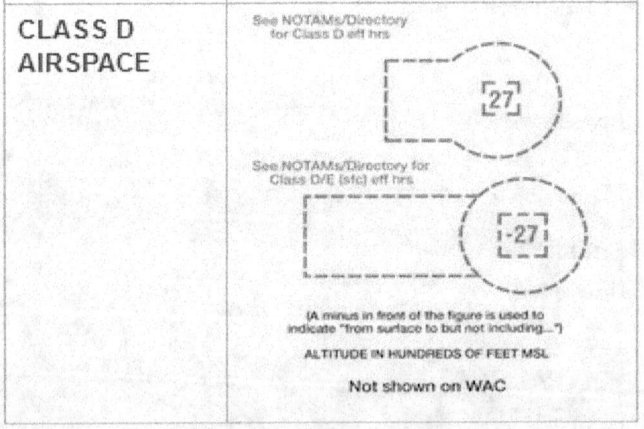

AIRSPACE CLASSIFICATION, OPERATING REQUIREMENTS AND FLIGHT RESTRICTIONS

CLASS E AIRSPACE

The limits of Class E airspace shall be shown by narrow vignettes or by the dashed magenta symbol. Individual units of designated airspace are not necessarily shown; instead, the aggregate lateral and vertical limits shall be defined by the following:

See NOTAMs/Directory for Class D/E (sfc) eff hrs

Airspace beginning at the surface (sfc) designated around airports...

See NOTAMs/Directory for Class E (sfc) eff hrs

Airspace beginning at 700 feet AGL...

See NOTAMs/Directory for 700' Class E eff hrs

Airspace beginning at 700 feet AGL that laterally abuts uncontrolled airspace (Class G)...

CLASS G

SO YOU WANNA BE A DRONE PILOT?

SPECIAL USE AIRSPACE *Only the airspace effective below 18,000 feet MSL is shown.*	P-56 or R-6401 or W-518 **PROHIBITED, RESTRICTED or WARNING AREA**
The type of area shall be spelled out in large areas if space permits.	ALERT AREA A-631 CONCENTRATED STUDENT HELICOPTER TRAINING **ALERT AREA**
	VANCE 2 MOA **MILITARY OPERATIONS AREA (MOA)**
MILITARY TRAINING ROUTES (MTR)	←IR292 Not shown on WAC
SPECIAL MILITARY ACTIVITY ROUTES (SMAR)	40 / 05 AGL 45 / 05 AGL
Boxed notes shown adjacent to route.	SPECIAL MILITARY ACTIVITY CTC MOBILE RADIO ON 123.6 FOR ACTIVITY STATUS

40 — Ceiling of SMAR in hundreds of feet MSL
05 AGL — Floor of SMAR in hundreds of feet AGL

AIRSPACE CLASSIFICATION, OPERATING REQUIREMENTS AND FLIGHT RESTRICTIONS

SPECIAL CONSERVATION AREAS

National Park, Wildlife Refuge, Primitive and Wilderness Areas, etc.

PAHRANAGAT NATIONAL WILDLIFE REFUGE

Not shown on WAC

NOAA Regulated National Marine Sanctuary Designated Areas

Flight operations below 1000' AGL over the designated areas within the Gulf of Farallones National Marine Sanctuary violate NOAA regulations (see 15 CFR 922).

SPECIAL AIRSPACE AREAS

SPECIAL FLIGHT RULES AREA (SFRA) RELATING TO NATIONAL SECURITY

Example: Washington DC

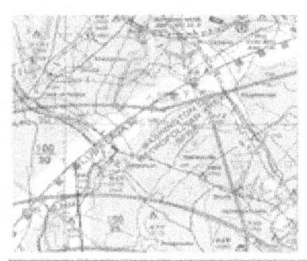

Appropriate notes as required may be shown.

Note: Delimiting line not shown when it coincides with International Boundary, projection lines or other linear features.

SO YOU WANNA BE A DRONE PILOT?

SPECIAL FLIGHT RULES AREA (SFRA)	CAUTION: Pilots should not attempt flight in the Grand Canyon Special Flight Rules area (GCN SFRA) below 18,000 feet using this chart as their primary navigational reference. Pilots intending to fly within the Grand Canyon SFRA should refer to the Grand Canyon VFR Aeronautical Chart for detailed information. Chart is available from the Federal Aviation Administration (phone 1-800-638-9912) or authorized agents.
TEMPORARY FLIGHT RESTRICTION (TFR) RELATING TO NATIONAL SECURITY *Example:* *Appropriate notes as required may be shown.*	CAUTION P-40 AND R-4009 EXPANDED BY TEMPORARY FLIGHT RESTRICTION. CONTACT AFSS FOR LATEST STATUS AND NOTAMS. Not shown on WAC
AIR DEFENSE IDENTIFICATION ZONE (ADIZ) *Note. Delimiting line not shown when it coincides with International Boundary, projection lines or other linear features.*	CONTIGUOUS U.S. ADIZ
NATIONAL SECURITY AREA *Appropriate notes as required may be shown.*	NOTICE FOR REASONS OF NATIONAL SECURITY PILOTS ARE REQUESTED TO AVOID FLIGHT BELOW 1200 MSL IN THIS AREA

AIRSPACE CLASSIFICATION, OPERATING REQUIREMENTS
AND FLIGHT RESTRICTIONS

The gray area is OK to fly in, the white area is restricted.
See the boundary? Keep looking until you can't unsee it.

| FLIGHT RESTRICTED ZONE (FRZ) RELATING TO NATIONAL SECURITY
Example:
Washington DC | 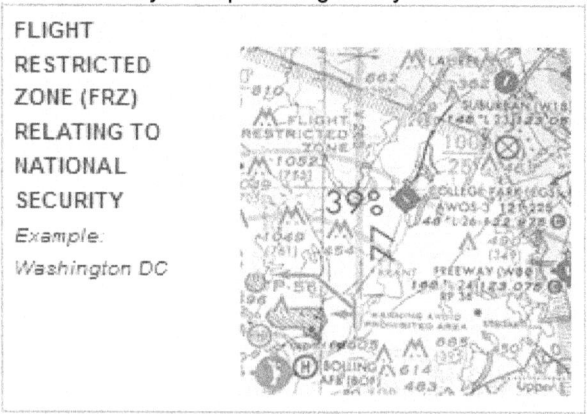 |

Navigational and Procedural Information

ISOGONIC LINE AND VALUE *Isogonic lines and values shall be based on the five year epoch magnetic variation model.*	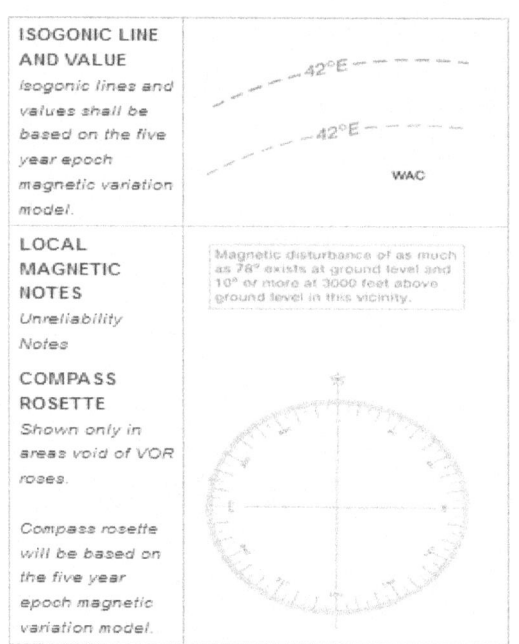
LOCAL MAGNETIC NOTES *Unreliability Notes*	
COMPASS ROSETTE *Shown only in areas void of VOR roses.* *Compass rosette will be based on the five year epoch magnetic variation model.*	

SO YOU WANNA BE A DRONE PILOT?

VFR CHECKPOINTS *Underline indicates proper name of VFR Checkpoint.*	Pictorial — STATE CAPITOL ■ SIGNAL HILL NORTHBROOK 113.0 Ch 77 OBK (R) LEWIS (Pvt) 9i89 - 27 Not shown on WAC
VFR WAYPOINTS *RNAV* *Stand-Alone* *Collocated with VFR Checkpoint*	GRANT VPXYZ NAME (VPXYZ) Not shown on WAC
OBSTRUCTION	1473 (394) bldg — Less than 1000' AGL — 1158 (553) stack 628 UC — Under Construction or reported and position / elevation unverified — 507 UC 3368 (1529) — 1000' AGL and higher — 2967 (1607) 2144 (389) — Wind Turbine — 1400 UC WAC

AIRSPACE CLASSIFICATION, OPERATING REQUIREMENTS AND FLIGHT RESTRICTIONS

HIGH-INTENSITY OBSTRUCTION LIGHTS

High-intensity lights may operate part-time or by proximity activation.

Less than 1000' AGL

1000' AGL and higher

Wind Turbine

Group Obstruction

WAC

WIND TURBINE FARMS

When highest wind turbine is unverified, UC will be shown after MSL value.

WAC

MAXIMUM ELEVATION FIGURE (MEF)

(see VFR Terms tab for explanation)

13⁵

WARNING AND CAUTION NOTES

Used when specific area is not demarcated.

WARNING
Extensive fleet and air operations being conducted in offshore areas to approximately 100 miles seaward.

CAUTION: Be prepared for loss of horizontal reference at low altitude over lake during hazy conditions and at night.

SO YOU WANNA BE A DRONE PILOT?

GROUP OBSTRUCTION

Symbol	Description	Symbol
1062 (227)	Less than 1000' AGL	1524 (567)
4977 (1432)	1000' AGL and higher	3483 (1634)
2889 (1217)	At least two in group over 1000' AGL	4892 (1573)
1164 (329) UC	Wind Turbines	1600

WAC

Chart Limits

OUTLINE ON SECTIONAL OF TERMINAL AREA CHART

— LOS ANGELES TERMINAL AREA —
Pilots are encouraged to use the Los Angeles VFR Terminal Area Chart for flights at or below 10,000'

Not shown on WAC

AIRSPACE CLASSIFICATION, OPERATING REQUIREMENTS
AND FLIGHT RESTRICTIONS

OUTLINE ON
SECTIONAL OF
INSET CHART

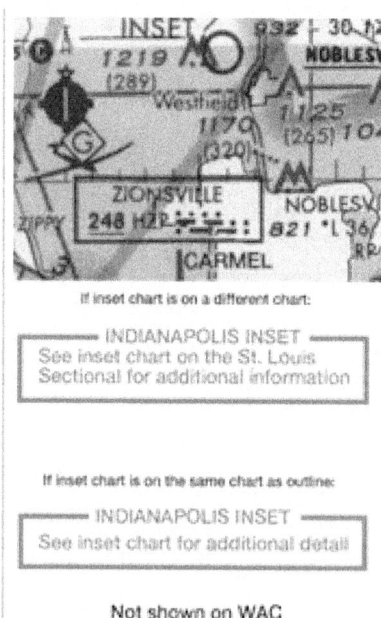

If inset chart is on a different chart:

─── INDIANAPOLIS INSET ───
See inset chart on the St. Louis
Sectional for additional information

If inset chart is on the same chart as outline:

─── INDIANAPOLIS INSET ───
See inset chart for additional detail

Not shown on WAC

SO YOU WANNA BE A DRONE PILOT?

Culture

RAILROADS	
Single Track	———┼———┼———┼———┼——— ———┼———┼———┼———┼——— WAC
Double Track	═══╪═══╪═══╪═══╪═══ ———┼———●———┼———●——— WAC
More Than Two Tracks	3 tracks ———╪═══╪═══╪═══╪———
Electric	electric ———┼———┼———┼———┼———
Non-operating, Abandoned or Under Construction	abandoned ———┼—— ——┼——— ——┼—

RAILROAD YARDS	
Limiting Track To Scale	railroad yard ———┼——⌒——┼———┼———
Location Only	railroad yard ■ ———┼———┼———┼———┼———

RAILROAD STATIONS	station station ——■┼———┼———┼—■—┼———

RAILROAD SIDINGS AND SHORT SPURS	———┼———┼⌒——┼———┼——— ╲

AIRSPACE CLASSIFICATION, OPERATING REQUIREMENTS AND FLIGHT RESTRICTIONS

ROADS Dual-Lane Divided Highway Category 1	═══════════════ ─────────────── WAC
Primary Category 2	─────────────── ─────────────── WAC
Secondary Category 2	───────────────
TRAILS Category 3 Provides symbolization for dismantled railroad when combined with label "dismantled railroad."	─ ─ ─ ─ ─ ─ ─ ─
ROAD MARKERS Interstate Route No. U.S. Route No. Air Marked Identification Label	▬▬▬▬▬ 80 ▬▬▬▬▬ ───── 60 ───── [13]
ROAD NAMES	LINCOLN HIGHWAY LINCOLN HIGHWAY WAC
ROADS UNDER CONSTRUCTION	under construction ─ ─ ─ ─ ─ ─ ─ ─

51

SO YOU WANNA BE A DRONE PILOT?

Hydrography

OPEN WATER	
INLAND WATER	
OPEN/INLAND WATER	
SHORELINES *Definite*	
Fluctuating	
Unsurveyed Indefinite	

AIRSPACE CLASSIFICATION, OPERATING REQUIREMENTS AND FLIGHT RESTRICTIONS

Under Construction	
STREAMS	
Perennial	
Non-Perennial	
Fanned Out	
Alluvial fan	
Braided	
Disappearing	
Seasonally	
Fluctuating	
with undefined limits	
with maximum bank limits, prominent and constant	
Sand Deposits in and along riverbeds	
WET SAND AREAS	
Within and adjacent to desert areas	

Relief

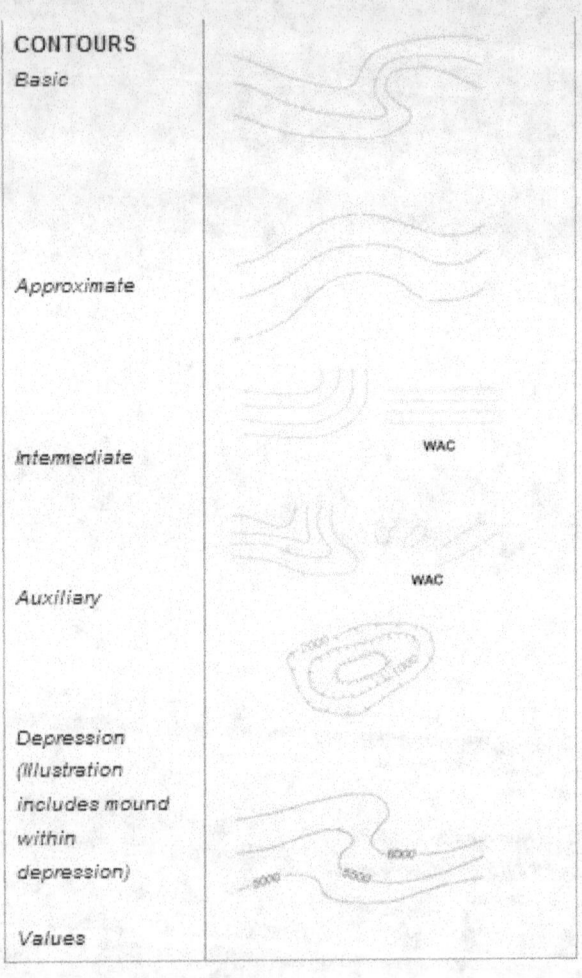

AIRSPACE CLASSIFICATION, OPERATING REQUIREMENTS AND FLIGHT RESTRICTIONS

SHADED RELIEF	
ROCK STRATA OUTCROP	rock strata
QUARRIES TO SCALE	quarry
STRIP MINES, MINE DUMPS AND TAILINGS *To Scale*	strip mine mine dump
CRATERS	
ESCARPMENTS, BLUFFS, CLIFFS, DEPRESSIONS, ETC.	
LEVEES AND ESKERS	levee

Flight Restrictions

Notices to Airmen (NOTAMs) are time-critical, often temporary, aeronautical information immediately published through National Notice to Airmen (NOTAM). This information is required for safe flight and is published at tfr.faa.gov and **https://pilotweb.nas.faa.gov/PilotWeb/**
Some reasons for a NOTAM:
- Hazards, such as air shows, parachute jumps, kite flying or rocket launches
- Flights by important people, such as heads of state
- Inoperable lights on tall obstructions
- Temporary erection of obstacles near airfields
- Flocks of birds flying through airspace (a NOTAM in this category is known as a BIRDTAM)

Dangerous flying situations:
Never fly under unmanned balloons because they have long, thin, invisible guide wires.

Inspecting another aircraft in flight.
This needs to be done carefully and consider: which pilot is in a position to direct the operation, area, direction and speed of intercept, aerodynamic effects, minimum safe separation distance, communication requirements, suitability of diverting distressed aircraft and emergency actions which would terminate intercept.

Precipitation static (P-static) – generated when the sUA flies through thunderstorms or airborne particles, like dust, ash or smoke. The negatively charged particles stick to the aircraft's skin, creating a huge static charge. This should be dissipated with static dischargers built into the airframe. The untreated static charge will discharge from the sUA causing communication interference, loss of video and loss of signal. Very dangerous.

Lasers - it is illegal to shine a laser at a plane. All laser sightings should be reported to the FAA. Laser sightings will be broadcast over the ATIS for one hour and

AIRSPACE CLASSIFICATION, OPERATING REQUIREMENTS
AND FLIGHT RESTRICTIONS

appropriate frequencies every five minutes for twenty minutes.

Smoke stacks and cooling towers produce dangerously unstable rising air. Sometimes it is invisible and can reach up to 1,000 feet above the top of the tower. It is best to stay well clear and upwind if possible. These hazards usually appear on charts.

Flying in the wire environment - This is considered everything under 1,000 feet, due to the high number of power lines and guide lines supporting towers. These wires are often very hard to see. Extra caution should be shown when you fly in this airspace.

Antenna Towers
Antenna towers and their guide wires are a threat because they can be very difficult to see. Support wires can extend out up to 1,500 feet, so 2,000 feet is the closest you should fly. New towers may not be on the charts yet.

The FAA expects you to know about and use the existing "flight operations" support structure. You are expected to know (not testable) 14 CFR 91:
Part 137 Agricultural aircraft operations
Part 139 Certification of airports
Part 141 Pilot schools
Part 142 Training centers
Part 145 Repair stations
14 CFR 99 Part 7 Special security instructions (What to do when the F16s show up to escort you, because you are flying in the WRONG place.)

This info can be found at **www.ecfr.gov**. Select "Title 14 Aeronautics and Space" and browse for the correct part number using the links.

Wildlife Strikes
All collisions with wildlife must be reported on "Bird/Other Wildlife Strike Report" found in the AIM and on the FAA

website for electronic submission. Birds migrate in the spring and fall and cause many collisions, especially ducks/geese and gulls. Many airports advise pilots of birds and other large animals in the runway.

You cannot land or fly anywhere controlled by the National Park Service, US Fish and Wildlife Service or US Forest Service and must fly at least 2,000 feet in the air. Don't fly here without special permission.

3a. Aviation Weather Sources

Intro
Aviation weather service is a concerted effort of the National Weather Service (NWS), Federal Aviation Administration (FAA), Department of Defense (DOD), other weather services and individuals to predict future weather. Weather reports and forecasts should be used for preflight planning and during the flight.

Surface Aviation Weather Observations are a network of government and private weather facilities producing continuous, up-to-date weather information. Automated Weather Observing Systems (AWOS) and Automated Surface Observing Systems (ASOS) contribute to the constant data input. The report includes: type of report, station ID, date and time, modifier when needed, wind, visibility, runway visual range (RVR), weather phenomena, sky condition, temperature/dew point, altimeter reading and remarks. Surface aviation weather observations are location specific, around an airport, and can be helpful to the RPIC.

Aviation Weather Reports
Aviation Routine Weather Report (METAR) is an international format you need to be familiar with.
1.Type of report. Routine METARs are released on a set schedule. SPECI METARs are special reports, released at any time, due to changing conditions, aircraft mishap or other critical need.

SO YOU WANNA BE A DRONE PILOT?

2. Station ID is a four letter code which always starts with a "K" in the continental US, Alaska begins with PA and Hawaii begins with PH. (KGGG - K for US and GGG for Gregg County Airport in Longview, Texas.)
3. Date and Time of Report is in six digits followed by the letter "Z". (161753Z) The first two digits are the day and the last four digits are the time, which is always in UTC. The "Z" reminds you it is Zulu time (UTC) and not local time.
4. Modifiers let you know if the report came from an automated source "AUTO" or if this report is a correction "COR". (METAR KGGG 161753Z COR)
5. Wind is reported as five digits. (14021KT) The first three digits are the direction the true wind is blowing and the last two digits are the speed in knots. The KT reminds you it is knots. (G26KT) after the speed means "gusting to 26 knots".
6. Visibility is reported in statute miles and fractions (¾ SM). (You need 3 statute miles to fly).
7. Weather is divided into qualifiers and phenomenon. (+TSRA BR – Heavy Thunder Storms, RAin and mist) The qualifiers for intensity and proximity are followed by the descriptor for the weather phenomenon. Intensity can be light (-), moderate ( ) or heavy (+). Nothing is shown for proximity if it is at airport. If weather is within the 5-10 mile vicinity, then "VC" is noted. Descriptors are used for precipitation and obscuration. Phenomena can be precipitation, obscurations or other things like squalls or funnel clouds. Start and end times and hail stone size are listed in "Remarks".
8. Sky condition is reported by amount, in eighths, height and type. Cloud bases are reported as three digits for hundreds of feet AGL. Towering Cumulus (TCU) and cumulonimbus (CB) are reported with height.
9. Temperature and dew point are reported in degrees Celsius (18/17). Negative numbers are preceded by "M" for minus.
10. Altimeter setting is reported in inches of mercury ("HG) as four digits, which ALWAYS follow "A". The remarks section is for "PRESRR" pressure rising rapidly and

AVIATION WEATHER SOURCES

"PRSFR" pressure falling rapidly.
11. Zulu time is a 24 hour clock for the whole world, designated by "Z" and centered in Greenwich, England.
12. Remarks, when used, begin with "RMK" and can include wind data, variable visibility, start and end times for phenomenon, pressure info, etc. (OCNL LTGICCG - OCcasioNaL LighTeninG In Clouds and from Cloud to Ground.)

Example: METAR KGGG 161753Z AUTO 14021G26KT 3/4SM +TSRA BR BKN008 OVC012CB 18/17 A2970 RMK PRESFR
Explanation: Routine METAR for Gregg County Airport for the 16th day of the month at 1753Z automated source. Winds are 140 at 21 knots gusting to 26. Visibility is ¾ statute mile. Thunderstorms with heavy rain and mist. Ceiling is broken at 800 feet, overcast at 1,200 feet with cumulonimbus clouds. Temperature 18 °C and dew point 17 °C. Barometric pressure is 29.70 "Hg and falling rapidly.

Aviation Forecasts
Forecasts are generated from observed weather. Your preflight planning should include one of these forecasts: TAF, FA – aviation area forecast, SIGMET- Significant Meteorological Information (SIGMET) used i7nflight, AIRMET- Airman's Meteorological Information or FB – forecast winds and temperatures aloft.

TAF – Terminal aerodrome forecast for five statute mile radius around (larger) airport, good for 24 to 30 hours. Updated regularly at 0000Z, 0600Z, 1200Z and 1800Z and uses the same abbreviations as METAR in the following order:
1. Type of report – forecast (TAF) or amended forecast (TAF AMD).
2. ICAO Station ID – same letters as METAR.
3. Date and time of origin – same six digit format as METAR.
4. Valid period dates and times – given in two four digit sets

(0812/0912). The first two digits of each set are the date and the last two are the time, so the eighth at noon (Z) until the ninth at noon (Z). 12 midnight start time is 00, 12 midnight end time is 24, so all day and night on the ninth is 0900/0924.

5. Forecast wind – shown as five digits followed by "KT"(to remind you the speed is in knots) 15011KT. The first three digits are the direction from true north and the next two are the speed. Our example shows the wind coming from SSE (150 degrees) at eleven knots.

6. Forecast visibility – shown in statute miles and fractions up to six miles. Everything greater than six miles is "P6SM".

7. Forecast significant weather- phenomena use the same abbreviations as METAR.

8. Forecast sky conditions – only CB clouds are forecast, shown the same as METAR.

9. Forecast change group – expected weather condition and time period. From "FM" is used for rapidly changing conditions within the hour, temporary "TEMPO" is used for temporary weather fluctuations less than one hour long.

10. PROB30 – percentage of probability that rain or thunderstorm will occur, not used for first six hours of the 24 hour forecast.

Qualifier		Weather Phenomena		
Intensity or Proximity 1	Descriptor 2	Precipitation 3	Obscuration 4	Other 5
– Light	MI Shallow	DZ Drizzle	BR Mist	PO Dust/sand whirls
Moderate (no qualifier)	BC Patches	RA Rain	FG Fog	SQ Squalls
+ Heavy	DR Low drifting	SN Snow	FU Smoke	FC Funnel cloud
VC in the vicinity	BL Blowing	SG Snow grains	DU Dust	+FC Tornado or waterspout
	SH Showers	IC Ice crystals (diamond dust)	SA Sand	SS Sandstorm
	TS Thunderstorms	PL Ice pellets	HZ Haze	DS Dust storm
	FZ Freezing	GR Hail	PY Spray	
	PR Partial	GS Small hail or snow pellets	VA Volcanic ash	
		UP *Unknown precipitation		

The weather groups are constructed by considering columns 1–5 in this table in sequence: intensity, followed by descriptor, followed by weather phenomena (e.g., heavy rain showers(s) is coded as +SHRA).
* Automated stations only

AVIATION WEATHER SOURCES

Example: TAF KPIR 111130Z 1112/1212 TEMPO 1112/1114 5SM BR FM1500 16015G25KT P6SM SCT040 BKN250 FM120000 14012KT P6SM BKN080 OVC150 PROB30 1200/1204 3SM TSRA BKN030CB FM120400 1408KT P6SM SCT040 OVC080 TEMPO 1204/1208 3SM TSRA OVC030CB

Explanation: Routine TAF for Pierre, South Dakota…on the 11th day of the month, at 1130Z…valid for 24 hours from 1200Z on the 11th to 1200Z on the 12th…wind from 150° at 12 knots… visibility greater than 6 SM…broken clouds at 9,000 feet… temporarily, between 1200Z and 1400Z, visibility 5 SM in mist…from 1500Z winds from 160° at 15 knots, gusting to 25 knots visibility greater than 6 SM…clouds scattered at 4,000 feet and broken at 25,000 feet…from 0000Z wind from 140° at 12 knots…visibility greater than 6 SM…clouds broken at 8,000 feet, overcast at 15,000 feet…between 0000Z and 0400Z, there is 30 percent probability of visibility 3 SM…thunderstorm with moderate rain showers…clouds broken at 3,000 feet with cumulonimbus clouds…from 0400Z…winds from 140° at 8 knots…visibility greater than 6 miles…clouds at 4,000 scattered and overcast at 8,000… temporarily between 0400Z and 0800Z…visibility 3 miles… thunderstorms with moderate rain showers…clouds overcast at 3,000 feet with cumulonimbus clouds…end of report (=).

Sky Cover	Contraction
Less than 1/8 (Clear)	SKC, CLR, FEW
1/8–2/8 (Few)	FEW
3/8–4/8 (Scattered)	SCT
5/8–7/8 (Broken)	BKN
8/8 or (Overcast)	OVC

Convective Significant Meteorological Information (WST)
Convective SIGMETs are reports issued for severe weather including tornadoes, hail larger than three quarters of an inch, thunderstorms with winds greater than 50 knots, embedded thunderstorms, lines of thunderstorms and thunderstorms with heavy precipitation. You need to check for these during flight planning.

The RPIC is required to be aware of the weather and visibility at time of flight. One way to get online flight weather is from: www.1800wxbrief.com You will need to create an account. Click the tab for UAS.

*NOTE: The phone based system is ONLY for manned aircraft pilots. RPICs must use internet.

You can also use the National Weather Service at **www.aviationweather.gov**, which is free and does not require registration. This site provides METARs and TAFs.

Weather Charts
Weather charts are graphic charts which show current or forecast fronts, high and low pressure areas, surface winds and pressures. These charts should be used for flight planning. The Surface Analysis Chart shows current surface weather and is published every three hours for the continental 48 states. This chart is comprised of reporting stations, which are shown. Weather Depiction Chart shows METAR info but do not include wind or pressure readings like surface analysis charts. Significant Weather Prognostic Charts are available from the surface to 24,000 feet (FL240) and are issued four times per day for flight planning.

3b. Effects of Weather

Two atmospheric characteristics have a major influence on flight: pressure and temperature.

Density Altitude
Dense air provides lower density altitude and improved aircraft performance. Less dense air provides higher density altitude and decreased performance. Dense, heavy air is lower and light air is higher. Air Density is affected by altitude, temperature and humidity. At constant temperature, doubling the pressure doubles the air density. At constant pressure, raising the temperature lowers the density and lowering the temperature raises the density. As altitude increases, temperature and pressure both decrease, having opposite effects upon air density, with pressure effects causing low density at high altitude. Low density altitude is near the ground and is dense and easy to fly through. High density altitude is way up high and less dense and a hazard to fly through for three reasons: internal combustion engines function less efficiently lowering power, propellers and jets function less efficiently lowering thrust, wing airfoils perform less efficiently lowering lift.

Because water vapor floats like a cloud, it is lighter than air. The more water in the air, the lighter it is. Wetter air is less dense and decreases performance. Humidity is the percentage of possible water vapor present in the air. Warm air can hold more water than cold air.

Performance
Performance is the ability of the aircraft to perform its mission. Performance is affected by takeoff and landing distance, rate of climb, ceiling, payload, range, speed, maneuverability, stability and fuel economy.

Climb Performance Factors
Climb Performance is the ability to create excess thrust or excess power and is affected by three primary factors: weight, altitude and configuration.

Weight has a large effect upon performance. More weight means a higher angle-of-attack (AOA), which increases the drag on the wings, which requires more power, thereby leaving less power available to climb.

As altitude increases, so does the power requirements, leaving less power available to climb.

Measurement of Atmospheric Pressure
Standard pressure, at sea level, is defined as 29.92 inches of mercury (Hg) at 59 degrees F (15°C). Standard Atmospheric Pressure can also be reported in millibars (mb) as 1,013.2 mb. Surface charts, pressure centers and hurricanes are reported in mb. All barometric pressures are reported at sea level. One inch of mercury is added for every 1,000 feet of elevation to correct to sea level. So, if you are 5,000 feet up, you need to add five inches of mercury to your readings.

Effects of Obstructions on Wind
Ground topography and large buildings can alter the flow of wind causing gusts and swirls. On the windward side of the mountain, the air is smooth and lifts the aircraft, but on the downwind side the air is turbulent and pushes the aircraft into the mountain. This can be very noticeable during takeoff and landing.

EFFECTS OF WEATHER

Low-Level Wind Shear
Wind shear is an abrupt, severe change in wind speed and/or direction. The aircraft can be pushed up, down or sideways and is especially dangerous when it happens near the ground. Low-level wind shear is found with passing fronts, thunderstorms and temperature inversions.

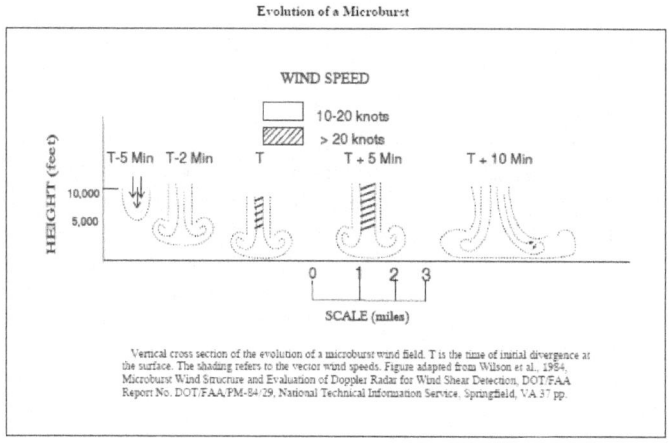

Evolution of a Microburst

Vertical cross section of the evolution of a microburst wind field. T is the time of initial divergence at the surface. The shading refers to the vector wind speeds. Figure adapted from Wilson et al., 1984, Microburst Wind Structure and Evaluation of Doppler Radar for Wind Shear Detection, DOT/FAA Report No. DOT/FAA/PM-84/29, National Technical Information Service, Springfield, VA 37 pp.

Microburst is the most severe type of low-level wind shear and is found when convective precipitation meets dry air at cloud's base. This looks like rain "hanging" in the air but only an intense downdraft hits the surface and spreads out in all directions. This causes both vertical and horizontal wind shear. Microbursts are usually 1-2 miles across and can last for 5-15 minutes producing downdrafts up to 6,000 feet per minute and shifting head/tail winds of 30-90 knots with turbulence. Wind shear is brief and usually not reported, so always be alert, especially around fronts and thunderstorms. Wind shear can cause you to crash or land short.

Atmospheric Stability
A stable atmosphere has no vertical motion and vertical disturbances are smothered. An unstable atmosphere allows vertical disturbances to grow into turbulence and convective activity, causing vertical clouds and severe weather.

Stability revolves around moisture and temperature. Cool, dry air is stable; warm, moist air is unstable.

Surface Heat
Different types of ground radiate heat at different rates creating turbulence. Plowed fields and parking lots affect the air above them differently, creating turbulence.

Inversion
Normally air rises, expands and cools. Sometimes a shallow layer of smooth stable air is trapped close to the ground, called an "inversion". The temperature of this inversion layer increases with altitude to the top of the layer. A humid inversion layer produces clouds, fog, smog and lower visibility. Two types of inversions: surface based found on clear cool nights when the ground cools the lower air more than the upper air and frontal inversions where warm air covers cold air or cold air slips under warm air.

Temperature/Dew Point Relationship
The dew point is the temperature where the air cannot hold any more water. The atmosphere is saturated with moisture. There are four ways this can happen: warm air can move over a cold surface, cold air and warm air can mix, night air cooled by the ground and warm air forced upward.

On cool, clear, calm nights the temperature of objects on the ground may drop below the dew point, resulting in dew

EFFECTS OF WEATHER

on these objects. If the temperature is below freezing, this will be seen as frost. Frost can be very dangerous to aircraft. The buildup of frost on a wing increases drag and disrupt air flow. Your sUA must be clean and frost-free before every flight.

Clouds

Cumulonimbus is the most dangerous cloud to fly near. They can be formed from warm air rising (air mass thunderstorm) or air rushing up mountains (orographic thunderstorms). Squall lines are nonfrontal bands of continuous cumulonimbus. Thunderstorms produce updrafts, downdrafts, hailstones, lightening, tornadoes and rain and can be very hazardous to safe flight.

Standing Lenticular Altocumulus Clouds form on the crests of waves created by barriers to the wind, like mountain tops. The clouds do not appear to move, so they are called "standing". They have smooth, polished edges and very high winds. Do not fly through these.

Unstable air has cumuliform clouds, showers, turbulence and good visibility. Stable air has stratiform clouds and fog, steady rain, smooth air and poor visibility.

A front forms when two different types of air masses meet. The temperature, humidity and wind can change quickly.

Plan flights over mountains carefully. Clouds can show you stable air (stratified clouds) and turbulent air (standing lenticular or rotary clouds.) Expect turbulence on the downwind side of the mountain.

Icing

Icing occurs when ice forms on an object and is a major hazard to flight. Icing is a cumulative hazard, the longer it happens, the worse it gets. Structural Icing occurs when the aircraft flies through moisture and the aircraft skin is below 0 C. Aerodynamic cooling can lower the wing temperature a few degrees. The build up of ice (accretion) destroying the airfoil is more hazardous than the weight of the ice. Airspeed is a strong non-meteorological factor. The aircraft may stall, roll or pitch.

Life cycle of a Thunderstorm
A thunderstorm goes through three stages: cumulus, mature and dissipating. The transition from one stage to the next is impossible to see. The cumulus stage looks like large puffy white clouds. Not all cumulus become thunderstorms, but all thunderstorms started as cumulus. Thunderstorms have a strong updraft from the surface to the top of the cloud and the cloud top can grow 3,000 feet per minute. Do not fly around here. Water drops are lifted up high where they can freeze, fall down, get larger and lifted back up again. The mature stage is reached when the cold downdraft mixes with the warm updraft and the rain drops are too big to lift up again. The rain falls with a strong cold downdraft. The wind hits the surface and spreads out into a "plow wind", behind the "first gust". Updrafts can reach 6,000 feet per minute and can create vertical shear with the down draft. The storms greatest intensity is reached. Very dangerous to flight. The dissipating stage sees the rain and downdrafts lessen until they stop. What's left is a harmless, fluffy white cloud.

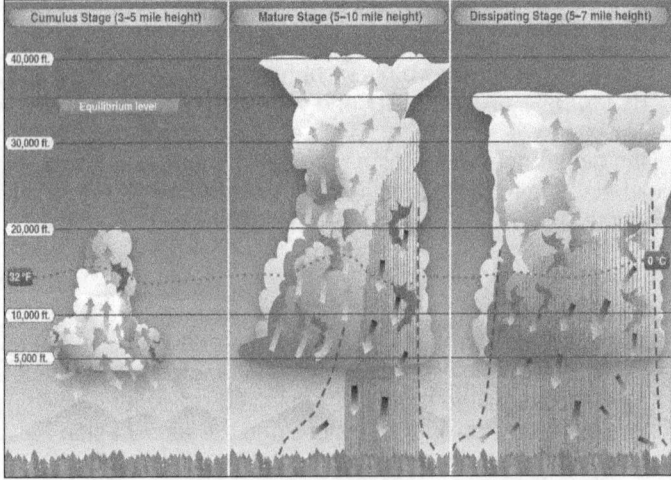

EFFECTS OF WEATHER

Lightning
Lightning is the visible electrical discharge produced by a thunderstorm. The discharge may be between the clouds, between the clouds and the air, between the clouds and the ground and between the ground and the clouds. Lightning is hazardous and should be avoided. The light can be temporarily blinding and lightning can disrupt radio signals.

Hail
Hail is frozen balls of precipitation produced by a thunderstorm. Hailstones can range from ¼ inch up to 4.5 inches and can cause serious damage. Hail is more common aloft, because it often melts before hitting the ground. Severe thunderstorms with strong updrafts produce large hail.

Ceiling
The aviation ceiling is the lowest layer of broken or overcast clouds or the vertical distance you can see into fog or haze. Broken clouds cover 5/8 to 7/8 of the sky, overcast covers the whole sky (8/8). The RPIC will find this info in their METAR.

Visibility
Visibility is the greatest horizontal distance that a prominent object can be seen with the naked eye. Where does the RPIC find this info for their preflight weather briefing?
The METAR. What is the minimum visible distance required to fly? 3 miles. If you can't see three miles, you cannot take off.

Air Masses
An air mass is a large body of air with uniform temperature and humidity which forms over a source region. The air masses move from their source, bump into each other and change. There are five types of air masses:
Continental Arctic – cold and dry,
Continental Polar – cold and dry,
Continental Tropic – hot and dry,

Maritime Polar – cool and moist,
Maritime Tropic – warm and moist,

Fronts

A front is the boundary or transition zone between air masses and is classified by the new air mass replacing the other, older air mass. Fronts can control weather for days or longer. Most weather occurs along the front. There are cold fronts, warm fronts, stationary fronts and occluded fronts (mixed warm and cold).

Fog

The only difference between fog and a cloud is that the base of fog is on the ground and by definition the base of the cloud is above the ground. Fog decreases visibility to less than 5/8 of a statute mile (1 kilometer). It does not fall to the ground like drizzle. Fog forms when the temperature and the dew point difference is less than 4 degrees F (2 C).

Tornado

A tornado is a rapidly rotating column of air hanging from a cumuliform cloud and touching the ground. It is called a funnel cloud when it doesn't touch the ground and a water spout when it touches water. Tornadoes can occur anywhere, but are common in the central and eastern US during spring afternoons and evenings. Usually they only last a couple minutes and travel a couple miles, but they can last much longer and travel much farther. The vortex can be between a couple of yards diameter and several miles. Tornadoes are classified on the Enhanced F Scale for wind damage from EF-0 for weak (65-85 mph) to EF-5 for violent with over 200 mile per hour winds. Most tornadoes are produced by supercell thunderstorms.

4. Small Unmanned Aircraft Loading

Intro
It is the RPIC's responsibility to check the weight and balance of their aircraft to ensure it is properly loaded. Follow the manufacturer's guidelines. Always consider the effect of overloading in case of an emergency situation. Listed max takeoff weight may not be attainable in all situations due to elevation, temperature and humidity. Other pre-takeoff factors are runway length, surface slope, surface wind and obstacles, which could all require the lightening of the load. Weight changes during flight, especially fuel burn, can have a negative effect on balance. Your sUA may become unstable when you jettison a load (deliver a package).

Weight
"The takeoff/climb and landing performance of an aircraft are determined on the basis of its maximum allowable takeoff and landing weights." Gravity pulls on an object at that object's Center of Gravity (CG). This location can change on your aircraft depending on loading. Ensure that the CG is located properly. Overloading affects the aircraft's performance, structure and stability and control.

The Center of Pressure (CP) is where all the aerodynamic forces of lift act on your aircraft. The CG should normally be in front of the CP for fixed wing aircraft.

You must understand the aerodynamic relationship between lift and weight. Lift is an upward force on the wing perpendicular to both wind and travel direction. When lift is greater than weight, the aircraft rises.

Stability
Stability is an aircraft design characteristic to return to stable flight after equilibrium is disturbed. Stability affects maneuverability and controllability. Controllability is the aircraft's response to the pilot's maneuvering. Maneuverability is impacted by weight, inertia, flight controls, structural strength and power.

Load Factors
The RPIC should understand the forces which act upon their aircraft, how to use these forces and the operating limits of their airframe. Load factor, measured in Gs (the force of gravity) is a proportion between lift and weight. Load factor is the amount of force required to move the aircraft from a straight line course.

Example: a load factor of 3 means the total load on an aircraft's structure is three times its weight. Since load factors are expressed in terms of Gs, a load factor of 3 may be spoken of as 3 Gs, or a load factor of 4 as 4 Gs.

Knowledge of load factors is important because it is possible to dangerously overload your aircraft, causing an increased load factor, which can increase stalling speed to possibly safe flight speeds.

Load factor in steep turns (in fixed wing aircraft)
During a coordinated turn, at constant altitude the load factor is a combination of centrifugal force and weight. For each bank angle, the higher the speed, the slower the Rate-Of-Turn (ROT). The load factor is very high over 50 degrees bank angle. At 80 degrees the load factor exceeds the 6Gs acrobatic aircraft can withstand.

SMALL UNMANNED AIRCRAFT LOADING

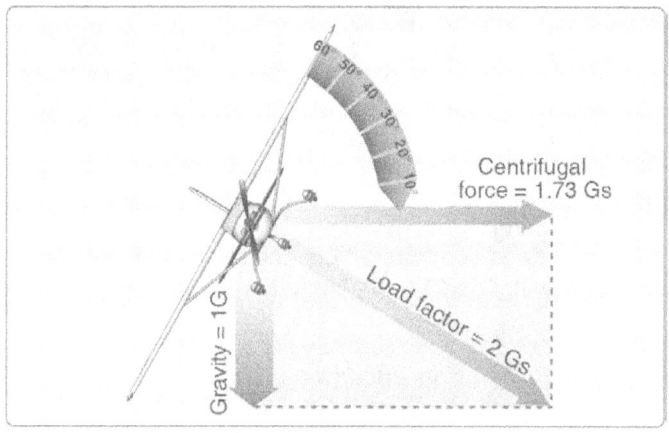

Load factors and stalling speeds
Any aircraft can be stalled at any speed simply by raising the nose, which increases the Angle-Of-Attack, (AOA). The smooth airflow over the wing breaks up, reduces lift and causes a stall. Stall speed increases in proportion to the square root of the load factor. An airframe which stalls at 50 knots can be made to stall at 100 knots by inducing a 4 G load factor. A steep turn or spiral can produce enough load factor to stall your sUA.

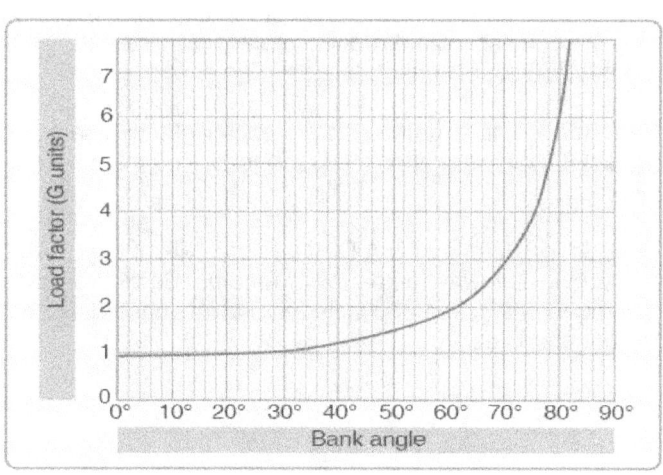

Weight and Balance (W&B)
Operating out of weight and balance can jeopardize flight safety, structural integrity and performance. The RPIC should frequently evaluate the aircraft's W&B and never operate with the CG outside of approved limits. Manufacturer's W&B limits must be followed.

Weight Control
Never overload your aircraft beyond recommended weight or you may not be able to generate enough lift to fly safely.

Lift
Lift is produced by an airfoil (wing) and is limited by design, angle-of-attack, air speed and air density.

Effects of Weight
Weight has a negative effect upon performance. Overloading is usually evident during takeoff. Performance deficiencies of an overloaded aircraft are higher takeoff speeds, longer runways, reduced rate and angle of climb, lower maximum altitude, shorter range, reduced cruising speed, reduced maneuverability, higher stall speed, higher landing speed and longer roll.

The RPIC must know the effects of weight on each aircraft they fly. Excess weight reduces safety margins and creates additional consequences in an emergency.

Performance data, gathered from each flight, can help predict the different effects experienced. You must keep a flight log.

The "So You Wanna Be A Drone Pilot? - Flight Log" is the perfect, flexible way to keep your records. Each book can hold up to 500 flights and includes preflight checklists and repair schedules.

5. Emergency Procedures

An inflight emergency is an <u>unexpected</u> situation that can have serious consequences. (If you fly with a broken sUA and have an emergency, the FAA will not deem this "unexpected".) An RPIC may deviate from **ANY** part of 14 CFR Part 107 to respond to an emergency. If you deviate from the rules during an emergency, you must report it to the FAA **WHEN ASKED**. (No ask, no tell.)

This has nothing to do with whether or not you caused someone or something harm. That is a different report and <u>must</u> be reported when damage is above a certain threshold.

Inflight Emergency
When is the RPIC responsible for safe flight? At all times. How does an RPIC ensure safe flight? Inspect the aircraft to ensure it is in a safe operating condition, no hazards to persons or property exist and all crew have been properly briefed on operational and emergency procedures.

It is the RPIC's responsibility to follow a preflight checklist to ensure the airframe is in safe condition before every flight. If a list does not exist for your airframe, adapt someone else's list or make your own.

When an inflight emergency happens, such as a battery fire, the RPIC may climb the sUA above 400 feet AGL to fly to a safe landing area. This would only be reported to the FAA if they ask. (I don't see how lifting a flaming battery hundreds of feet in the air could be safe, but it's the FAA's example, so you may see it again.)

Emergency Planning and Communication
Flight operations and emergency procedures must be discussed with all crew, including visual observers (VO) and non-licensed flight control operators, prior to takeoff. You are permitted to use any kind or radio, WiFi or other communication device to aid you. The FAA may request statements from everyone involved if there is an emergency.

Keep collateral damage to people and things to a minimum when exercising emergency procedures.

Lithium Batteries
Many sUA use lithium batteries which could catch fire and/or explode if handled improperly, especially during storage and transportation. Always inspect your batteries to ensure they are free of cuts, bulges and leaks. Batteries can be damaged during a sUA crash. Always follow manufacturer's suggested practices when handling, charging and storing batteries. Consider using a special "fire-proof" battery bag for storing and charging your batteries. Never let batteries get banged around. Ensure spare battery terminals are taped over and cannot contact metal objects.

Battery Fires
Most lithium batteries consist of multiple battery cells encased in plastic. If one cell ruptures and catches fire, the other cells will rupture, catch fire and possibly explode if nothing is done. The proper thing to do is to knock down the flames with halon or any water fire extinguisher and then cool the batteries with lots of water. If you do not run sufficient non-alcoholic liquid over the hot batteries, they will ignite again. The wrong type of fire extinguisher will trap heat in the batteries and cause them to explode. Halon or water based extinguishers only. Do not try to move burning batteries into a fire-proof bag, it is too

EMERGENCY PROCEDURES

dangerous.

Frequency spectrums
Many sUA communicate with the command station through the 2.4 GHz and/or 5.8 GHz radio frequency bands. The problem is because many wireless phones and computer networks also use these same spectrums and can cause interference. Many sUAS use 5.8 Ghz to control the aircraft and 2.4 GHz to transmit video and photos. WiFi uses both of these spectrums, so they can get crowded. Always use the manufacturer's recommended procedures when available.

Both 2.4 and 5.8 Ghz are considered line-of-sight frequencies. A building or a tree could cause interference.

The Global Positioning System could fail for a number of reasons, including loss of auxiliary power. This is another reason you must fly within line-of-sight.

"Loss of Control" and "Flyaway" are two of the problems associated with radio frequency interference and loss of GPS.

6. Crew Resource Management (CRM)

Intro
It is the RPIC's job to manage the crew, hardware and software while maintaining safety.

Crew Resource Management entails situational awareness, proper allocation of tasks, avoiding overwork in self and others and effectively communicating with all members of the crew, such as VOs and people manipulating the controls of the sUAS.

CRM can be improved through better: communication procedures, communication methods and task management.

Chapter 10, Aeronautical Decision-Making covers the topic of CRM in more detail.

7. Radio Communication Procedures

Intro
The RPIC is not expected to communicate over radio frequencies, but should be monitoring them to be aware of other air traffic. The RPIC is expected to understand "aviation language" to enhance their "situational awareness when operating in the NAS."

Ensure you know the phonetic alphabet (the real one, not the one from television).
Alpha, Bravo, Charlie, Delta, Echo, Foxtrot, Golf, Hotel, India, Juliet, Kilo, Lima (lee-mah), Mike, November, Oscar, Papa, Quebec (Keh-bec), Romeo, Sierra, Tango, Uniform, Victor, Whiskey, Xray, Yankee, Zulu.

Traffic Advisory Practices at Airports without Operating Control Towers
Always be alert, especially around Class G airports without an operating control tower. Some pilots may not announce their arrival and departure, but most do, and the RPIC needs to be monitoring this frequency. Pilots use three methods to communicate when no tower is operating: flight service station (FSS), universal communications (UNICOM) and self-announce broadcast. UNICOM provides automated weather, radio check and airport advisories and the frequency is published in the Airport Facility Directory and approach charts.

Understanding Communication on a Common Frequency
Airport advisories are broadcast over the Common Traffic Advisory Frequency (CTAF) via UNICOM, MULTICOM, FSS or a tower frequency for airports without an operating tower. Use MULTICOM frequency 122.9 at airports with no tower, FSS or UNICOM.

Recommended Traffic Advisory Practices
The RPIC must be familiar with traffic patterns, radio procedures and radio lingo (not "Breaker one nine..."), but is not expected to communicate with manned aircraft near non-towered airports.

The first frequency to check near non-towered airports is UNICOM, usually on 122.8, but check the charts in busy areas. If there is no tower, no UNICOM and no other frequency listed, try MULTICOM on 122.9. Again check the Sectional or Chart Supplement.

A manned aircraft approaching a non-towered airport will "broadcast-in-the-blind" from 10 miles out, as it approaches, lands and until it is clear of the runway. The pilot will announce the airport where he intends to land at the beginning and end of each broadcast. This broadcasting is recommended, but not required. The RPIC must always be alert for other air traffic.

Aircraft Call Signs
14 CFR part 107 requires RPIC to have permission to fly in controlled airspace around airports. You should have a radio to monitor the proper frequencies. You should never transmit over the radio unless it is an emergency.

The RPIC must learn aviation lingo. Calls signs are one form of lingo. Every aircraft's registration number in America begins with "N", such as N123AB. This is pronounced November, One, Two, Three, Alpha, Bravo. Small aircraft replace the "N" with their manufacturer or model (for heavier aircraft), such Cessna 123 AB, or Citation 123AB. Commercial airlines use their company call name and the flight number, such as "Southwest 711" for Southwest Airlines flight 711. Your thousand dollar sUA crashing a commercial airliner is one of the FAA's big fears. Don't be that RPIC.

Altitude
Up to but not including 18,000 feet MSL say each thousand's digit, then "thousand", then the hundred's digit, if needed, then "hundred". 12,000 => "One, Two Thousand"; 12,500 => "One, Two Thousand Five Hundred". At and above 18,000 feet (where oxygen is required) say "Flight Level" and the thousands and hundreds digits. 18,000 feet MSL (FL 180) => "Flight Level One Eight Zero".

Direction
Use three digits for bearing, course, heading and wind from magnetic compass. Say, "True" when using true North. Compass course 009 => "zero zero niner"; true course 090 => "zero niner zero true"; magnetic heading 100 => "heading one zero zero"; wind direction 220 => "wind two two zero".

Speeds
Each digit followed by "knots" for everyone but ATC controllers, who are too busy to say "knots", so they just say the digits. Speed 87 => "eight seven knots". Controller might say to you, "Reduce speed to five zero."

Time
All FAA time uses a 24-hour clock set in Coordinated Universal Time (UTC), designated by "Z" for zulu. Use the word "local" if using local time. 0920 UTC => "zero niner two zero zulu". You can convert UTC to local time by adding hours. New York standard time adds five hours, California adds eight, Alaska nine and Hawaii ten hours. Subtract one hour for daylight savings time.

8. Determining the Performance of Small Unmanned Aircraft

Intro
The RPIC must know the operational performance data for their sUA, to include takeoff, climb, range, endurance, descent and landing. Use the manufacturer's data if available, otherwise use published data for your aircraft from other pilot's and build your own database.

Effect of Temperature on Density
Increasing the temperature decreases the density and vise versa. Air density decreases with altitude.

Effect of Humidity (Moisture) on Density
Wet air is less dense (lighter) than dry air. The moisture percentage is called "relative humidity." Humidity is a minor influence on density altitude and performance.

9. Physiological Factors (Including Drugs and Alcohol) Affecting Pilot Performance

Intro
14 CFR part 107 forbids the unsafe operation of a sUAS by the RPIC, visual observer or person manipulating the controls. It is the RPIC's responsibility to ensure that no crew member is impaired by alcohol, drugs or over-the-counter medication. Part 107 forbids serving as any member of the crew if alcohol was consumed within 8 hours, if a person is under the influence of alcohol, has a blood alcohol concentration of .04 or greater or is using a drug that affects the person's mental or physical capabilities. The RPIC must ensure that crew members have mental and/or medical conditions, such as epilepsy/PTSD/Bipolar under control.

Physiological/Medical Factors that Affect Pilot Performance
The RPIC should be aware of hyperventilation, stress, fatigue, dehydration, heatstroke and the effects of drugs and alcohol.

Hyperventilation is rapid and deep breathing leading to loss of carbon dioxide from the blood. Anxiety makes it worse. Symptoms include blurry vision, unconsciousness, lightheaded or dizziness, tingling, hot and cold flashes and muscle spasms. Treatment is slow, steady breathing, breathing into a paper bag or speaking out loud.

Stress is the body's way of dealing with physical and psychological demands. Stress can cause the body to release hormones (like adrenaline) and increase metabolism. Blood sugar, heart rate, respiration, blood pressure and perspiration increase. "Stressor" is the thing that causes you stress. Stressors include noise or vibration (physical stress), fatigue (physiological stress) and interpersonal issues (psychological stress).

Stress can be short term (acute) or long term (chronic). Acute stress is an immediate threat and causes the "fight or flight" response. A healthy person can deal with acute stress. Continued acute stress can lead to chronic stress. Chronic stress presents a steady, intolerable burden with which the person cannot cope, causing performance to drop. Nonstop psychological pressure including loneliness, finance, relationships and work can result in chronic stress. The RPIC must ensure the crew is free from chronic stress. Crew members who suffer from chronic stress should see a doctor.

Fatigue frequently contributes to pilot error. Symptoms include decreased attention, concentration, coordination and communication. This lowers your ability to make decisions. Physical fatigue comes from loss of sleep or exercise and physical work. Mental fatigue comes from stress and extended thinking. Acute fatigue is short term, occurs every day and is cured by rest and a good night's sleep. Skill fatigue is a special kind of acute fatigue which disrupts timing and field of perception. With timing disruption the pilot performs each activity separately instead of continuously. Perception disruption means the pilot focuses on the center and ignores the edges, resulting in loss of accuracy and motor control. Acute fatigue can be caused by mild hypoxia (loss of oxygen), physical stress, psychological stress, loss of physical energy from psychological stress and sustained psychological stress. Acute fatigue can be prevented and cured by proper diet and sleep. No crew member should operate a sUAS with acute fatigue. Get proper rest before each flight.

PHYSIOLOGICAL FACTORS AFFECTING FLIGHT

Chronic fatigue has psychological roots, extends over a long time and results from high levels of stress, though it can be caused by disease. Chronic fatigue is not cured by diet and sleep and requires a doctor's treatment. Chronic fatigue leads to weakness, tiredness, heart palpitations, loss of breath, headaches, irritability, bowel problems, general aches and pains and eventually, mental illness. No crew member should be operating a sUAS with chronic fatigue, they should see a doctor.

Dehydration is the critical loss of the body's water and can be caused by hot temperatures, wind, humidity and diuretic drinks (tea, coffee, alcohol and caffeinated beverages.) Symptoms are headache, fatigue, cramps, sleepiness and dizziness. The first symptom is fatigue which impairs physical and mental performance. Flying your sUA during summer's heat or at high altitudes can increase your risk of dehydration.

As a rule of thumb, drink two to four quarts of water per 24 hours to prevent dehydration. If you do not replace your fluids you can experience fatigue, dizziness, weakness, nausea, tingling in hands and feet, abdominal cramps and extreme thirst. Don't wait until you are thirsty to drink water, use flavoring if you want and limit your intake of diuretics.

Heatstroke is the body's inability to control its temperature. It may start with dehydration, but is often not recognized until complete collapse. For severe heat conditions, drink one quart per hour.

Drugs
The FAA does not reference specific medications or illnesses.

There are two points to remember:
1.No one can serve as a sUAS crew member if they have any medical condition, or are taking any drugs, which would prevent them from passing a regular pilot's medical

exam.
2. "14 CFR part 107 prohibits the use of any drug which affects a person's faculties in a way contrary to safety."

Check your fitness before every flight by performing the "IMSAFE" survey. Check you and your crew for Illness, Medication, Stress, Alcohol, Fatigue and Emotion.

Don't forget about over-the-counter medicines, many of which cause drowsiness or other impairments.

Code section 91.19 forbids carrying narcotics, marijuana, depressant and/or stimulant drug or substance on a civil aircraft without FAA approval.

Alcohol
Code section 91.17 lays down the law and forbids crewmembers from:
1) Consuming alcohol within eight hours of flying;
2) Being under the influence of any alcohol or drug that could affect your senses in an unsafe way;
3) Having a blood alcohol level of 0.04 or higher.

"Even in small amounts, alcohol can impair judgment, decrease sense of responsibility, affect coordination, constrict visual field, diminish memory, reduce reasoning ability, and lower attention span. As little as one ounce of alcohol can decrease the speed and strength of muscular reflexes, lessen the efficiency of eye movements while reading, and increase the frequency at which errors are committed. Impairments in vision and hearing can occur from consuming as little as one drink."

You are still impaired when you are hung over! "Eight hours, bottle to throttle," is an old Navy pilot's saying and it still goes for visual observers and all people touching the sUAS controls.

PHYSIOLOGICAL FACTORS AFFECTING FLIGHT

Drug and Alcohol Testing
If you refuse to take a drug or alcohol test, or refuse to "furnish results" of a drug or alcohol test, your RPIC license can be suspended or revoked. If you are found guilty of ANY drug or alcohol offense, your RPIC license can be suspended for one year.

Drug and Alcohol Conviction
If you are applying for your RPIC license and have a drug or alcohol offense, you may have to wait up to one year from conviction.

Fitness For Flight
An RPIC cannot operate a sUAS if they know of any medical or physical condition which would disqualify them attaining a flight medical certificate. Some of these include alcoholism, drug addiction, epilepsy, psychosis, myocardial infarction, angina pectoris and diabetes requiring medical control. Temporarily disqualifying conditions include acute infections, anemia and peptic ulcers.

Vision
The RPIC should "understand about the eyes and how they function", because vision is the most important of the five senses for flight.

Be aware of the blind spot in each eye where the optic nerve joins the eyeball. There are no rods or cones here, so there is no ability to see. This is only an issue when vision is obstructed in one eye.

It takes your eyes time to adjust to the dark. Do not let night blindness hinder the safety of your flight. Proper night vision requires maximum oxygen intake.

To scan properly start at the top and look left to right to left in 30 degree arcs, pause for a second or two at each turn and overlap the arcs ten degrees. Off-center viewing is also useful for RPICs. Keep the sUA in your peripheral vision as you scan the air around it.

SO YOU WANNA BE A DRONE PILOT?

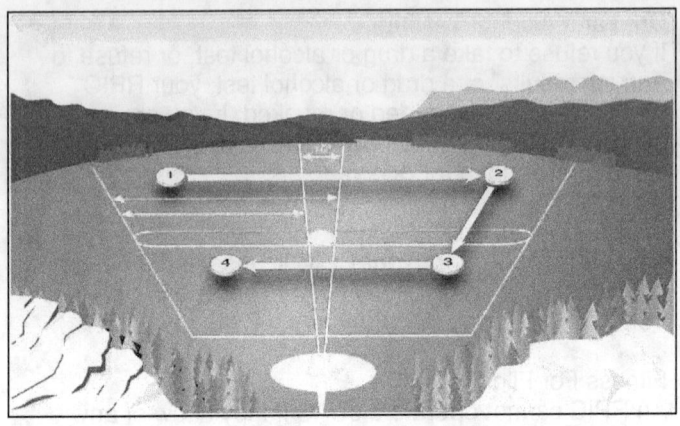

The Pilot's Handbook details optical illusions caused by the terrain or atmosphere, often seen by pilots when landing a plane. The RPIC needs three miles of visibility to fly, so many of the atmospheric issues should not be present.

10. Aeronautical Decision-Making (ADM) and Judgment

Intro
ADM is a systematic approach to determine the best course of action, based on current info. Over eighty percent of aviation accidents are caused by humans with half occurring during takeoff and landing. Proper ADM could prevent some of these accidents. ADM can be used to assess risk and manage stress. Personal attitudes and decision-making can be improved through knowledge and practice.

The airline industry invented ADM more than 25 years ago to decrease the number of accidents caused by humans. Crew Resource Management (CRM) training uses everything available, including human resources, hardware and information to improve ADM.

Good judgment can be taught. ADM provides a structured, systematic way to analyze changes during a flight and project how these changes might affect safety.

Straight from the FAA:

"A key element of risk decision-making is determining if the risk is justified."

"Steps for good decision-making are:
1. Identifying personal attitudes hazardous to safe flight.
2. Learning behavior modification techniques.

3. Learning how to recognize and cope with stress.
4. Developing risk assessment skills.
5. Using all resources.
6. Evaluating the effectiveness of one's ADM skills."

Risk Management
The purpose of risk management is to identify safety hazards and mitigate their risks. Six steps in risk management are: ID hazards, Asses risks, Analyze controls, Make control decisions, Use controls, Monitor results. Always ensure results don't produce unforeseen risk. Good decision making is a result of experience and education. Direct learning is when you experience the lesson for yourself (the hard way), indirect learning is when you observe someone else learning the hard way. Always remember four principles of risk management: never accept unnecessary risk, make risk decisions at appropriate level, accept risk when benefits outweigh danger and integrate risk management into all planning.

Crew Resource Management (CRM) and Single-pilot Resource Management (SRM)

Many CRM principles have been applied to single-pilot aircraft to develop SRM. SRM is the ability to manage all available resources, prior to and during a flight, to ensure a safe result and includes ADM, risk management, task management, automation management, controlled flight into terrain and situational awareness. Situational awareness is maintained by managing the aircraft's automation, control and navigation. SRM helps pilots gather and analyze information so they can make safe decisions.

Hazard and Risk

A hazard can be a real or perceived condition or event that causes a pilot to asses the possible impact(s). The pilot's assessment of the hazard's impact is the risk. Different pilots see hazards differently.

Hazardous Attitudes and Antidotes

Proper attitude is as important to flying as good health. Attitude is your personal response to people and situations. Five attitudes have been identified as hazardous to decision making: anti-authority, impulsivity, invulnerability, macho and resignation.

Hazardous attitudes can be corrected through personal effort. The first step is to recognize the hazardous attitude, next label the hazardous attitude as such and finally apply the correct "antidote". Antidotes need to be remembered automatically, every time a hazardous attitude creeps in.
Anti-authority: "Don't tell me!" => Follow the rules, they are usually right.
Impulsivity: "Do it quickly!" => Not so fast. Think first.
Invulnerability: "It won't happen to me!" => It could happen to me.
Macho: "I can do it!" => Taking chances is foolish.
Resignation: "What's the use?" => I'm not hopeless and I can make a difference.

Risk
Every pilot needs to constantly assess risk and determine the course of action to mitigate this risk. Single RPICs have no one to confer with about risk and are more vulnerable than a full crew. It is important for single RPICs to do the IMSAFE checklist: Illness, Medication, Stress, Alcohol, Fatigue and Emotion. The PAVE acronym is perfect for single RPICs to do preflight planning: Pilot-in-command, Aircraft, enVironment and External pressure. Each RPIC needs to have their own minimums for each PAVE element, below which they will not fly. For the "P", the RPIC should do the IMSAFE acronym. The "A" for Aircraft needs to be the right one for the mission and within the comfort level of the RPIC. The en"V"ironment includes the weather, terrain and airspace. Know the forecast, ceiling and visibility. Evaluate the terrain. Check for Temporary Flight Restrictions in your airspace. "E"xternal pressures include desire to impress someone, a pilot's general "goal-completion" attitude and refusing to say "No" because of pride. (Unable to say, "I don't know how to do that.") External pressures must be managed because they can cause the RPIC to ignore other risks. Personal Standard Operating Procedures (SOPs) provide a great way to handle the external pressures of flight.

Risk assessment consists of two parts, likelihood of occurrence and severity. These form the two sides of the risk matrix.

You, the RPIC must define the risk assessment and acceptance criteria, how you designate authority and how you determine who is responsible for risk management decision making. Risk acceptability should be evaluated using a risk matrix. AC-107-2 Appendix A shows a couple of examples and provides details how to construct a color-coded risk assessment chart. One generic example follows. The unacceptable is colored red, mitigation is yellow and acceptable is green.

AERONAUTICAL DESCION MAKING

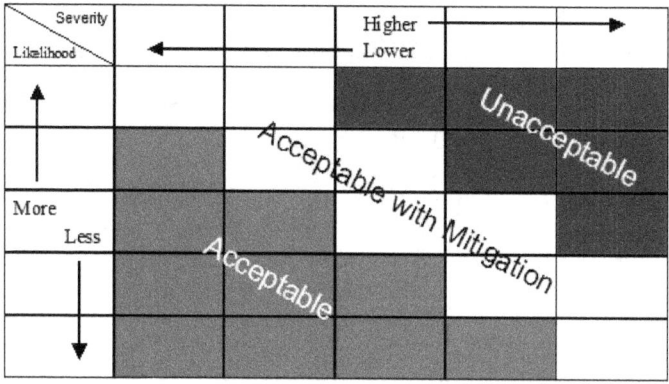

Human Factors
More than 70% of aircraft accidents are caused by the human factors of fatigue, complacency and stress. Human Factors Science studies how pilots, ATC and aviation mechanics use aviation systems and services. It studies how the humans act, how the machines react and how to make the results better.

The Decision-Making Process
Decision-making is the root of ADM and SRM skills and involves both risk management and risk intervention. Risk management and risk intervention help the RPIC identify hazards, assess the risks, analyze the controls, make a control decision, use the controls, monitor the results. There are several mnemonics to help you make a decision, such as the 5 Ps, 3P and DECIDE - Detect, Estimate, Choose, Identify, Do, Evaluate.

Automatic decision-making takes place when you don't have time to run through a list and weigh risks. The expert finds the first workable choice and then modifies it as the situation develops. The constant monitoring and refining of actions produces a workable outcome. This type of automatic decision-making gets better with experience and training.

Foreseeing Risk
The RPIC is expected to be able to identify and foresee hazards by asking, "What if?" Identify the hazard, determine the odds of occurrence and severity of the hazard, develop ways to mitigate the risk and verify mitigation does not cause new hazards.

Reducing Risk
Risk analysis should include Root Cause Analysis (RCA). RCA studies WHY certain risks are assigned certain levels. You do not need to identify every risk, just the major ones that you do not have a plan for. The more you fly, the more risk mitigation plans you will create. You are on your way to reducing risk.

Controlling Risk
Once hazards and risks are fully understood, risk controls must be designed and implemented. These can be additional or changed procedures, additional or modified equipment, the addition of VOs, or whatever else it takes to mitigate risk.

Residual and Substitute Risk
Residual risk remains after you have performed mitigation. This risk is evaluated. If the risk is now greater, this is called "substitute risk, where the cure is worse than the disease." Risk management is a continuous cycle of actions, monitoring and more actions and monitoring to reach a safe conclusion.

Operational Pitfalls
Experienced pilots have some common pitfalls:
Peer Pressure – poor decisions due to potential emotional response from peers
Mindset – refusal to change
Get-there-itis – single-minded attitude which disregards safety
Duck-under syndrome – flying below the minimum, because there is always a built-in safety margin
Sound running – flying by the ground when you should be using instruments

AERONAUTICAL DESCION MAKING

Continuing VFR flight in IR conditions – similar to sound running, but higher up
Getting behind the aircraft – pilot is constantly surprised by events, continuously responding
Loss of positional or situational awareness – not sure where your aircraft is
Operating without adequate fuel reserves – Ignoring minimum requirements and not planning properly
Descent below the minimum en route altitude – ducking under the en route portion of IFR flight
Flying outside the envelope – overestimating the aircraft and your own skills
Neglect of flight planning, preflight inspections and checklists – this will bite-you-in-the-butt if you get investigated by the FAA. You have been warned.

Stress Management
Everyone gets stressed, it's OK and even healthy. Performance increases with a little stress, maxes out with more stress and collapses with too much stress. Decision-making during flight is stressful. Ensure you manage your daily stress levels too.

Stressors include environmental (vibration, noise), physiological (tired, hungry) and psychological (personal problems).

Use of Resources
Informed decisions come from using ALL available resources. The time to use a resource contributes or detracts from its usefulness. The FAA expects RPICs to check the "B4UFly" app or a current chart to aid in decision-making.

Situational Awareness
Situational awareness requires understanding all flight related factors and their possible future impact. The five fundamental areas of safety risk are: flight, pilot, aircraft, environment and type of mission. Do not fixate on only one factor and become distracted. Fatigue, stress and overwork can contribute to a loss of situational awareness.

Workload management requires proper planning. Experienced pilots can foresee times of high workload and prepare when there is less to do. If possible monitor ATIS, Automated Surface Observing System (ASOS), Automated Weather Observing System (AWOS) and Common Traffic Advisory Frequency (CTAF). The first effect of work overload is working harder but getting less done. This leads to concentrating on only one task, ignoring other data inputs and making faulty decisions. The proper thing to do is slow down and prioritize items.

The ten biggest causes of pilot-related accidents:
1. Poor planning.
2. Failure to maintain speed.
3. Failure to maintain direction control.
4. Improper level off.
5. Failure to see and avoid obstructions
6. Failure to manage fuel.
7. Poor inflight decision making.
8. Misjudgment of speed and distance.
9. Poor terrain selection.
10. Improper use of flight controls.

The FAA publishes a manual on ADM, AC 60-22 Aeronautical Decision Making and a manual to teach Risk Management, H-8083-2.

11. Airport Operations

Intro
An airport is a place on land or water intended for the takeoff and landing of aircraft. These aircraft can be helicopters, seaplanes or tilt-rotor. The airport encompasses all buildings, facilities and rights-of-way designed for the operation and storage of aircraft. The RPIC must be aware of approach corridors, taxiways, runways and helipads and yield right-of-way to all other aircraft, even if they are on the ground. The RPIC is FORBIDDEN to interfere in manned aircraft operations! Example: You cannot hover 200 feet over a runway, even if the planes can fly under you. You would create a hazard.

Types of Airports
There are two types of airports, towered and non-towered broken down into three categories: civil (public use), military/Federal Government (military, NASA, etc.) and private (not open to the public).

Towered airports have an operating control tower and air traffic control (ATC) to provide safe routing of air traffic. Non-towered airports may have a tower that isn't operating or have no tower and do not require two-way radio communications. For safety and situational awareness, monitor the CTAF (Common Traffic Advisory Frequency) which may be on Universal Integrated Community (UNICOM), MULTICOM, FSS or tower frequency.

Runways

Runways have a line painted down the middle and a number which is the runway's clockwise approach direction from magnetic North. Runway markings are white. Taxiways and holding positions are yellow. Parallel runways are designated "L" for left, "C" for center and "R" for right. The runway aiming point and touchdown zone markers help pilots land.

Relocated runway threshold - ten foot wide white bar across runway with yellow arrow heads point to the bar all the way across.

Displaced threshold - ten foot wide white bar across runway with white arrow heads point to the bar all the way across.

Runway safety area – grassy area around runways.

Runway safety area boundary sign – yellow with black markings.

Runway holding position sign – white characters outlined in black on red background.

Runway holding position marking – two solid and two dashed yellow lines across runway.

Runway distance remaining sign - black background with white numbers.

Runway designation marking – degrees clockwise from magnetic north and a center line.

Taxiways have a center line and runway holding positions whenever they intersect a runway. Directions may be painted on the taxiway with a yellow background and black letters. Surface holding position signs have a red background with black outline and white numbers.

Traffic Patterns

Non-towered airports use a centrally located visual indicator to show wind direction, landing direction, landing strip and traffic pattern. Know pattern altitude. Most planes will enter the pattern at pattern altitude from the middle of the runway and make left turn to the downwind leg. Complete turn to final approach at least one quarter mile from runway. The traffic pattern looks like a big oval racetrack of planes.

AIRPORT OPERATIONS

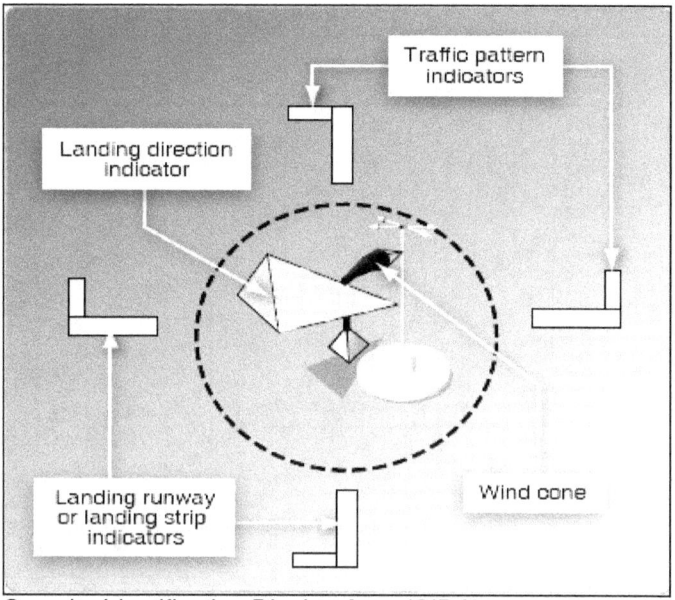

Security Identification Display Area (SIDA)
This is a limited access area, usually around the airport ramp, requiring a badge issued in compliance with CFR 49 Part 1542. Contact airport authorities if you are unsure of the SIDA location. Signs should be posted. Do not enter!

Sources of Airport Data
Any RPIC flying near an airport should be aware of the current data for that airport such as communication frequencies, services available, closed runways and construction. Four common sources of this info are: aeronautical charts, Chart Supplement, Notices to Airmen and Automated Terminal Information Service (ATIS).

The "Chart Supplement" is a detailed airport reference. It used to be seven books, but now is a downloadable file from the FAA website and provides the info on all public airports, heliports and seaplane ports. This information is not easily shown on charts, such as airport hours of operation, types of fuel available, runway widths, lighting codes, etc.

SO YOU WANNA BE A DRONE PILOT?

CHART SUPPLEMENT

26   **ALABAMA**

BIRMINGHAM INTL (BHM) 4 NE UTC -6(-5DT) N33°33.83' W86°45.14'   ATLANTA
650 B S4 **FUEL** 100LL, JET A OX 1, 2 LRA ARFF Index C   H-6K, 9A, L-14H
RWY 06-24: H12002X150 (ASPH-GRVD) S-175, D-205, DT-350 HIRL CL   IAP, AD
  RWY 06: ALSF2, TDZL. PAPI(P4L)—GA 2.8° TCH 39'.
  RWY 24: MALSR. PAPI(P4L)—GA 3.0° TCH 50'. Thld dsplcd 1200'. Tree. 0.5% down.
RWY 18-36: H7100X150 (ASPH-GRVD) S-75, D-170, DT-240 MIRL
  RWY 18: PAPI(P4L)—GA 3.2° TCH 52'. Ground.
  RWY 36: REIL. Trees.
AIRPORT REMARKS: Attended continuously. Bird activity invof all rwys. Normal dep point for Rwy 24 at numbers located at Twy A6. Twy F between twys G and B restricted to acft weighing 100,000 pounds or less. Twy N restricted to acft weighing 204,000 lbs or less. Twy M restricted to acft 75,000 lbs or less. Twy G restricted to acft 65,000 lbs or less. MALSR Rwy 24 controlled by twr but ops unmonitored. South ramp clsd to transient tfc permanently. Flight Notification Service (ADCUS) avbl. NOTE: See Land and Hold Short Operations Section.
WEATHER DATA SOURCES: ASOS (205) 591-6172. WSP.
COMMUNICATIONS: ATIS 119.4   **UNICOM** 122.95
  ANNISTON FSS (ANB) TF 1-800-WX-BRIEF. NOTAM FILE BHM.
  RCO 122.2 123.65 (ANNISTON FSS)
® **APP/DEP CON** 127.675 (231°-049°) 123.8 (050°-230°)
  TOWER 119.9 118.25   **GND CON** 121.7   **CLNC DEL** 125.675   **PRE-TAXI CLNC** 125.675
AIRSPACE: CLASS C svc continuous ctc APP CON
RADIO AIDS TO NAVIGATION: NOTAM FILE ANB.
  VULCAN (H) VORTAC 114.4   VUZ   Chan 91   N33°40.21' W86°53.99'   129° 9.8 NM to fld. 750/02E.   HIWAS.
  MC DEN NDB (HW/LOM) 224   BH   N33°30.68' W86°50.74'   057° 5.6 NM to fld. NOTAM FILE BHM.
  ROEBY NDB (LOM) 394   RO   N33°36.46' W86°40.73'   235° 4.6 NM to fld. NOTAM FILE BHM.
  ILS 110.3   I-BHM   Rwy 06. CLASS IIE.   LOM MC DEN NDB.
  ILS/DME 109.5   I-ROE   Chan 32   Rwy 24. CLASS IE.   LOM ROEBY NDB.
  ILS/DME 111.3   I-BXO   Chan 50   Rwy 18.   (LOC only).
  ASR

BLACKWELL FLD (See OZARK)

BLOOD N31°49.82' W86°06.33'   NOTAM FILE TOI.   NEW ORLEANS
  NDB (MHW/LOM) 365   TO   070° 5.1 NM to Troy Muni.   L-18F

BOGGA N33°32.06' W85°55.88'   NOTAM FILE ANB.   ATLANTA
  NDB (LOM) 211   AN   050° 4.9 to Anniston Metropolitan.

BOLL WEEVIL N31°20.21' W85°59.00'   NOTAM FILE ANB.   NEW ORLEANS
  NDB (MHW) 352   BVG   121° 4.8 NM to Enterprise Muni. Unmonitored Sun and Mon 0500-1200Z‡.   L-18F, 19A
  Unusable byd 20 NM.

BRANTLEY N31°33.71' W86°17.58'   NOTAM FILE ANB.   NEW ORLEANS
  NDB (MHW) 410   XBR   120° 34.4 NM to Cairns AAF. NDB unmonitored Sun and Mon 0500-1200Z‡.   L-18F, 19A

AIRPORT OPERATIONS

Notices to Airmen (NOTAM)
NOTAMs provide the most time-critical aeronautical information, especially for temporary events. They can affect your decision of when and where to fly. See them at https://pilotweb.nas.faa.gov/PilotWeb/ or tfr.faa.gov

Automated Terminal Information Service (ATIS)
A looped broadcast of local weather and other non-control information at busy airports. Updated at least once per hour with runway info, ATC procedures and airport construction info. Each broadcast is given a unique "alphabet letter" name to distinguish them (Alpha, Bravo, Charlie). The Chart Supplement US shows which airports use ATIS.

Aeronautical Charts
Charts are like "maps for pilots". The two charts used for visual flight are Sectionals and VFR Terminal Area. You can download free charts (Digital Products) or order paper charts from the FAA website at **www.aeronav.faa.gov**

Sectional Charts are the most commonly used chart by pilots. They have a 1:500,000 scale which works out to one inch equaling about 8 statute miles. The chart includes airport info, navigational aids, airspace and topography. The chart legend shows how to read the chart, what each symbol means and ATC frequencies. Sectionals are revised semiannually inside the continental US and annually outside the US.

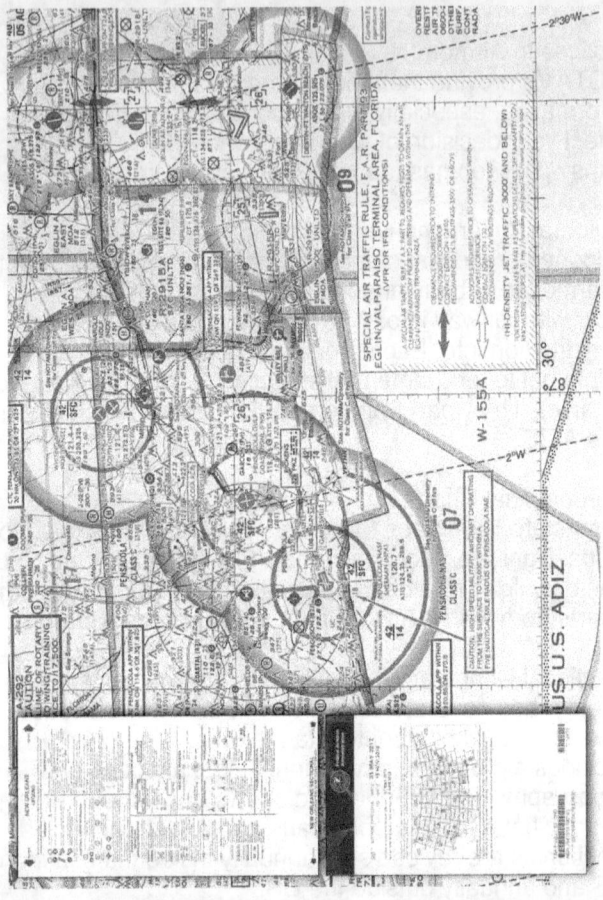

Latitude and Longitude (Meridians and Parallels)
The equator is an imaginary line circling the earth equal distance from the North and South poles and is zero degrees latitude. Parallels of latitude are circles that are parallel to the equator and are used to measure north and south latitude. (They look like the rungs of "ladder" (latitude), climbing up the earth.) The continental US is located between 25 and 49 degrees North latitude. Meridians of longitude run from the North Pole to the South Pole and are perpendicular to the equator. The

AIRPORT OPERATIONS

Prime Meridian which runs through Greenwich, England is the zero line for measuring east and west. This is also the zero line for time correction, Zulu time. The continental US is between 67 and 125 degrees West longitude. Any place on the Earth can be located using latitude and longitude. Washington D. C. is at approximately 39 degrees North latitude and 77 degrees West longitude.

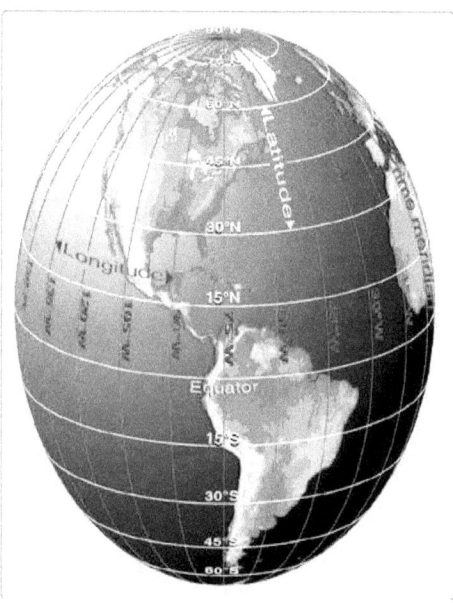

Variation

Variation exists because true north and magnetic north are about 1,300 miles apart. The variation is expressed as degrees east or west to correct to true north. There is also magnetic variation caused by geological conditions. Isogonic lines connect points of equal variation and are shown as magenta lines on aeronautical charts and are labeled east and west with a number like +5 or -5. The line between them, where there is no variation, is called the agonic line.

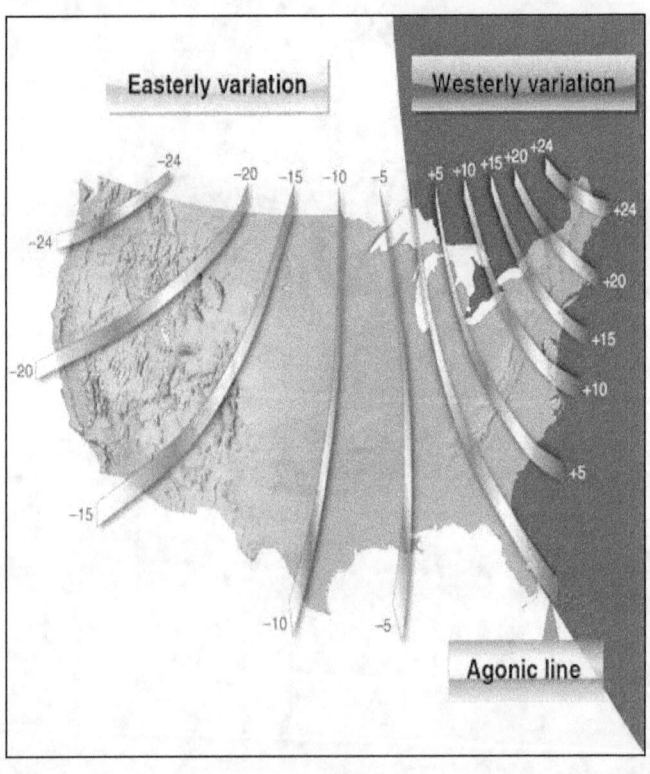

12. Maintenance and Preflight Inspection Procedures

Intro
Section 107.15 requires the RPIC to perform a preflight safety inspection before every flight.

Benefits of Recordkeeping
The FAA is serious about recordkeeping! You are expected to maintain a hard copy or digital copy, of all inspections, maintenance, preventative maintenance, repairs and alterations to the airframe, control station, payload and any other component required for safe flight.

Proper record keeping demonstrates RPIC responsibility establishing airworthiness prior to each flight. Records help establish component service life as well as failure rates.

The FAA states: "Maintenance and inspection recordkeeping provides retrievable empirical evidence of vital safety assessment data defining the condition of safety-critical systems and components supporting the decision to launch."

Translation in American: "Your records show you checked EVERYTHING before EVERY takeoff."

*NOTE: If you ever need to file an accident report with the FAA, they will want to see ALL of your records!

Basic Maintenance

sUAS maintenance includes any and all changes and inspections to the aircraft. This information should be kept in a log and follow manufacturer's recommendations. If there are no manufacturer's scheduled maintenance instructions then you need to develop your own. Document each repair and modification from normal flight and record time-in-service for each part. Over time you can establish a reliable maintenance schedule. If unscheduled maintenance needs to be performed for any reason, including software updates, the RPIC is not to fly until the issue is resolved. It is important that all maintenance is completed before each flight, according to the manufacturer's instructions or industry best practices. Any part that cannot be repaired must be replaced.

Your sUAS mechanics should be licensed by the manufacturer and/or have aeronautical experience and certificates.

Preflight Inspection

The RPIC is responsible for performing a safety inspection of the sUAS before every flight. This inspection should follow manufacturer's procedures or an inspection routine developed by you. You can use industry guidelines and other aircraft's inspection procedures to develop your own. Your inspection should include the complete sUAS to ensure all components are safe to fly. Part 107 recommends the RPIC visually or functionally check:

1. Visual condition of the sUAS and its components.
2. Airframe structure, including undercarriage, flight control surfaces and linkages.
3. Proper registration markings.
4. Movable control surfaces including airframe attachment points.
5. Servo motors including attachment points.
6. Propulsion system – power plant, propellers, rotors, ducted fans, etc.
7. Verify adequate power for all sUAS components.
8. Avionics – control link transceiver, communication/navigation equipment and antennas.

MAINTENANCE AND PREFLIGHT INSPECTIONS

9. Calibrate UAS compass prior to flight.
10. Control link transceiver, communication/navigation data link transceiver and antennas.
11. Display panel is functioning properly.
12. Check ground support equipment-takeoff/landing gear
13. Ensure that proper control communication is established to the sUA.
14. Check correct movement of control surfaces using control station.
15. Check onboard navigation and communication links.
16. Check flight termination system.
17. Check fuel for correct type and quantity.
18. Check battery levels for aircraft and control station.
19. Check that any equipment is securely attached.
20. Verify communication with the sUA and that the sUAS has acquired at least four GPS satellites.
21. Start and inspect propellers for imbalance or irregularity.
22. Verify controller header and altitude.
23. Note any obstructions that are in your flight path.
24. At controlled low altitude, fly near any interference and recheck controls and stability.

Preflight damage and the proper responses from AC 107-2, Appendix C.
1.Structural or skin cracking Further inspect to determine scope of damage and existence of possible hidden damage that may compromise structural integrity. Assess the need and extent of repairs that may be needed for continued safe flight operations.
2.Delamination of bonded surfaces Further inspect to determine scope of damage and existence of possible hidden damage that may compromise structural integrity. Assess the need and extent of repairs that may be needed for continued safe flight operations.
3.Liquid or gel leakage Further inspect to determine source of the leakage. This condition may pose a risk of fire resulting in extreme heat negatively impacting aircraft structures, aircraft performance characteristics, and flight duration. Assess the need and extent of repairs that may

be needed for continued safe flight operations.

4. Strong fuel smell Further inspect to determine source of the smell. Leakage exiting the aircraft may be present and/or accumulating within a sealed compartment. This condition may pose a risk of fire resulting in extreme heat negatively impacting aircraft structures, aircraft performance characteristics, and flight duration. Assess the need and extent of repairs that may be needed for continued safe flight operations.

5. Smell of electrical burning or arcing Further inspect to determine source of the possible electrical malfunction. An electrical hazard may pose a risk of fire or extreme heat negatively impacting aircraft structures, aircraft performance characteristics, and flight duration. Assess the need and extent of repairs that may be needed for continued safe flight operations.

6. Visual indications of electrical burning or arcing (black soot tracings, sparking) Further inspect to determine source of the possible electrical malfunction. An electrical hazard may pose a risk of fire or extreme heat negatively impacting aircraft structures, aircraft performance characteristics, and flight duration. Assess the need and extent of repairs that may be needed for continued safe flight operations.

7. Noticeable sound (decibel) change during operation by the propulsion system Further inspect entire aircraft with emphasis on the propulsion system components (motors, propellers, etc.) for damage and/or diminished performance. Assess the need and extent of repairs that may be needed for continued safe flight operations.

8. Control inputs not synchronized or delayed Discontinue flight and/or avoid further flight operations until further inspection and testing of the control link between the ground control unit and the aircraft. Ensure accurate control communications are established and reliable prior to further flight to circumvent possible loss of control resulting in the risk of a collision or flyaway. Assess the need and extent of repairs that may be needed for continued safe flight operations.

9. Battery casing distorted (bulging) Further inspect to determine integrity of the battery as a reliable power

MAINTENANCE AND PREFLIGHT INSPECTIONS

source. Distorted battery casings may indicate impending failure resulting in abrupt power loss and/or explosion. An electrical hazard may be present, posing a risk of fire or extreme heat negatively impacting aircraft structures, aircraft performance characteristics, and flight duration. Assess the need and extent of repairs that may be needed for continued safe flight operations.

10. Diminishing flight time capability (electric powered propulsion systems) Further inspect to determine integrity of the battery as a reliable power source. Diminishing battery capacity may indicate impending failure due to exhausted service life, internal, or external damage. An electrical hazard may be present, posing a risk of fire or extreme heat negatively impacting aircraft structures, aircraft performance characteristics, and flight duration. Assess the need and extent of repairs that may be needed for continued safe flight operations.

11. Loose or missing hardware/fasteners Further inspect to determine structural integrity of the aircraft and/or components with loose or missing hardware/fasteners. Loose or missing hardware/fasteners may pose a risk of negatively impacting flight characteristics, structural failure of the aircraft, dropped objects, loss of the aircraft, and risk to persons and property on the grounds. For continued safe flight operations, secure loose hardware/fasteners. Replace loose hardware/fasteners that cannot be secured. Replace missing hardware/fasteners.

Preflight Requirements
The FAA states that, "The RPIC must:
1. Conduct an assessment of the operating environment. The assessment must include at least the following:
- Local weather conditions,
- Local airspace and any flight restrictions,
- The surface location of persons and property
- Other ground hazards.
2. Ensure that all persons directly participating in the sUA operation are informed about the following:
- Operating conditions,

- Emergency procedures,
- Contingency procedures,
- Roles and responsibilities of each person involved in the operation,
- Potential hazards.

3. Ensure that all control links between the Control Station (CS) and the sUA are working properly. For example, before each flight, the RPIC must determine that the sUA flight control surfaces necessary for the safety of flight are moving correctly through the manipulation of the sUA CS. If the RPIC observes that one or more of the control surfaces are not responding correctly to CS inputs, then the RPIC may not conduct flight operations until correct movement of all flight control surface(s) is established.

4. Ensure there is sufficient power to continue controlled flight operations to a normal landing. One of the ways that this could be done is by following the sUA manufacturer's operating manual power consumption tables. Another method would be to include a system on the sUAS that detects power levels and alerts the RPIC when remaining aircraft power is diminishing to a level that is inadequate for continued flight operation.

5. Ensure that any object attached or carried by the sUA is secure and does not adversely affect the flight characteristics or controllability of the aircraft.

6. Ensure that all necessary documentation is available for inspection, including the RPIC's remote pilot certificate, aircraft registration (if required), and Certificate of Waiver (CoW) (if applicable)."

Now, if all risks are mitigated, you may take off.

Authorized Maintenance
Normally only certified aircraft mechanics can work on aircraft. SUA do not have certified mechanics yet, so use mechanics certified by you manufacturer if possible. You must keep meticulous records.

Appendix 1 Step-by-Step To Get Your License

This is for non-pilot applicants, without a Part 61 flight certificate.

1. Pass the initial aeronautical knowledge test at an approved knowledge testing center.
2. Complete FAA Form 8710-13, Remote Pilot Certificate Application online at iacra.faa.gov/iacra. You must create an account.
3. Click "Start New Application".
4. Application type – Select "Pilot".
5. Certifications – Select "Remote Pilot".
6. Click "Start Application".
7. Verify the information on the Application Process Page is correct and click the green "Save and Continue" button at the bottom of the page.
8. Answer the English Language and Drug Conviction questions on the Supplementary Data page. Add explanations if needed. Click the green "Save and Continue" button.
9. The Basis of Issuance page opens. Input your photo ID info, preferably from your driver's license. Enter the 17-digit knowledge test exam ID in the Search box. It can take up to 72 hours for test results to appear in IACRA. When the test appears, click the green Associate Test button. Click the green "Save and Continue" button.

10. The "Review and Submit" page will open. Answer the denied certificate question and review the Pilots Bill of Rights, Privacy Act and your application.

11. Sign the Pilots Bill of Rights Acknowledgment form.

12. Sign and complete the application.

13. Your temporary certificate will be available in IACRA in about 7 days.

14. Your permanent certificate will be mailed to you.

If you have a Part 61 flight certificate and a current 24 month flight review, you do not need to take the full test, just the Part 107 section. See AC 107-2 section 6.4.2 for more info.

APPENDIX 2 ABBREVIATIONS

Abb./Acronym Definition
14 CFR Title 14 of the Code of Federal Regulations
AC Advisory Circular
ACS Airman Certification Standards
ADDS Aviation Digital Data Services
ADIZ Air Defense Identification Zone
ADM Aeronautical Decision-Making
AFM Airplane Flight Manual
AFS Flight Standards Service
AGL Above Ground Level
AIRMET Airman's Meteorological Information
AOA Angle of Attack
ATC Air Traffic Control
ATD Aviation Training Device
CB Cumulonimbus
CFA Controlled Firing Areas
CFR Code of Federal Regulations
CG Center of Gravity
CP Center of Pressure
CRM Crew Resource Management
CS Control Station
CTAF Common Traffic Advisory Frequency
CTP Certification Training Program
DPE Designated Pilot Examiner
DVFR Defense VFR

EMS Emergency Services
FAA Federal Aviation Administration
FADEC Full Authority Digital Engine Control
FDA Federal Drug Administration
FDC Flight Data Center
FL Flight Level
FRZ Flight Restriction Zone
FS Flight Service
FSDO Flight Standards District Office
IAP Instrument Approach Procedures
ICAO International Civil Aviation Organization
IFR Instrument Flight Rules
IR Instrument Routes (sectional charts)
ISA International Standard Atmosphere
LAA Local Airport Advisory
MAP Missed Approach Point
MDA Minimum Descent Altitude
MEL Minimum Equipment List
MFD Multi-functional Displays
MOA Military Operation Areas
MSL Mean Sea Level (the "above" is assumed)
MTR Military Training Route
NACG National Aeronautical Charting Group
NASA National Aeronautics and Space Administration
NAS National Airspace System
NM Nautical Miles
NOAA National Oceanic and Atmospheric Administration
NOTAM Notice to Airmen
NSA National Security Area
OTC Over-the-Counter
PART 107 - The section of 14 CFR which deals with sUA flight
PAVE PIC – Aircraft – enVironment – External pressures
POH Pilot's Operating Handbook
RPIC Remote Pilot in Command
SAO Special Area of Operation
SIGMET Significant Meteorological Information
SOP Standard Operating Procedures

APPENDIX 2 ABBREVIATIONS

sUA small Unmanned Aircraft
sUAS small Unmanned Aircraft System
TCU Towering Cumulus
TFR Temporary Flight Restrictions
TN True North
TRSA Terminal Radar Service Area
TUC Time of Useful Consciousness
UA Unmanned Aircraft
UNICOM Aeronautical Advisory Communications Stations
UTC Coordinated Universal Time
VLOS Visual Line Of Sight
VFR Visual Flight Rules VR Visual Routs (sectional charts)
VO Visual Observer
W&B Weight and Balance
WST Convective Significant Meteorological Information

Test Tips

When taking a knowledge test, please keep the following points in mind:

• Carefully read the instructions provided with the test.

• Answer each question in accordance with the latest regulations and guidance publications.

• Read each question carefully before looking at the answer options. You should clearly understand the problem before trying to solve it.

• After formulating a response, determine which answer option corresponds with your answer. The answer you choose should completely solve the problem.

• Remember that only one answer is complete and correct. The other possible answers are either incomplete or erroneous.

• If a certain question is difficult for you, mark it for review and return to it after you have answered the less difficult questions. This procedure will enable you to use the available time to maximum advantage.

• When solving a calculation problem, be sure to read all the associated notes. If two sources are given, such as a chart and a legend, be sure to check them both for the information you need.

• For questions involving use of a graph, you may request a printed copy that you can mark up while figuring out your answer. This copy and all other notes and paperwork must be given to the testing center upon completion of the test.

• Answer every question because there is no penalty for wrong answers. Use the "Review" button to be sure you answered them all.

SAMPLE UAS EXAM

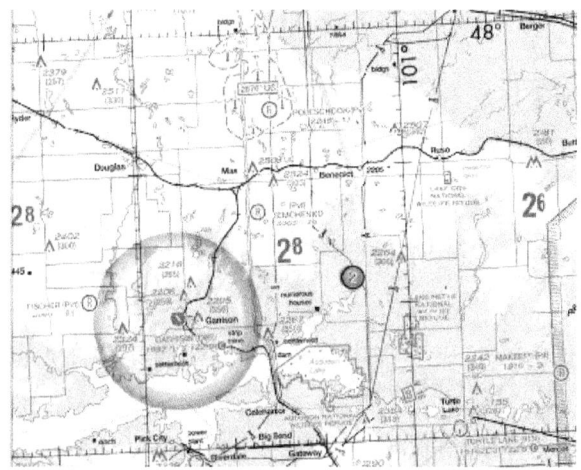

1. What airport is located at approximately 47 degrees, 40 minutes N latitude and 101 degrees, 26 minutes W longitude?

A) Mercer County Regional Airport
B) Semshenko Airport
C) Garrison Airport

2. What does the line of latitude at area 4 measure?
A) The degrees of latitude east and west of the Prime Meridian.

SO YOU WANNA BE A DRONE PILOT?

B) The degrees of latitude north and south of the equator.
C) The degrees of latitude east and west of the line that passes through Greenwich, England.

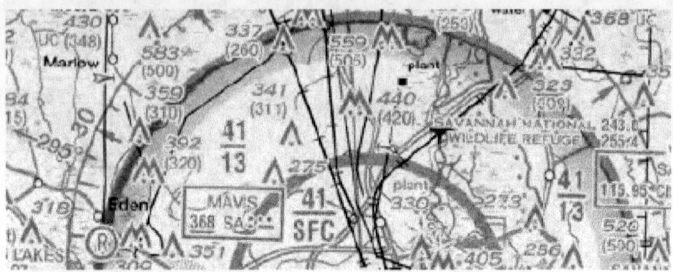

3. What is the floor of the Savannah Class C airspace at the shelf area (outer circle)?
A) 1,300 feet AGL
B) 1,300 feet MSL
C) 1,700 feet MSL

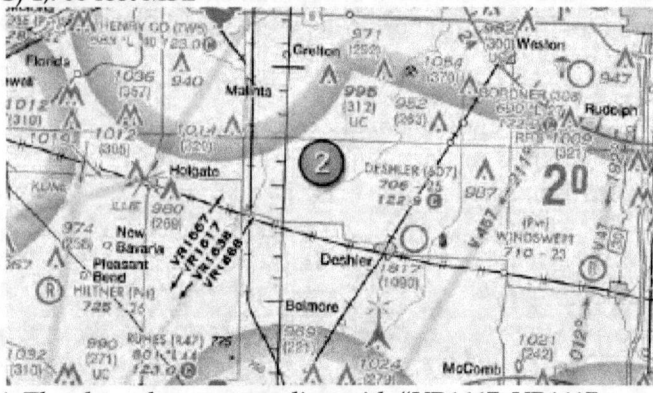

4. The chart shows a gray line with "VR1667, VR1617, VR1638 and VR1668." Could this area present a hazard to the operations of small UA?
A) No, all operations will be above 400 feet.
B) Yes, this is a Military Training Route from the surface to 1,500 AGL.
C) Yes, the defined route provides traffic separation to manned aircraft.

5. According to 14 CFR Part 107, the remote pilot in command (PIC) of a small unmanned aircraft planning to operate within Class C airspace
A) must use a visual observer.
B) is required to file a flight plan.
C) is required to receive ATC authorization.

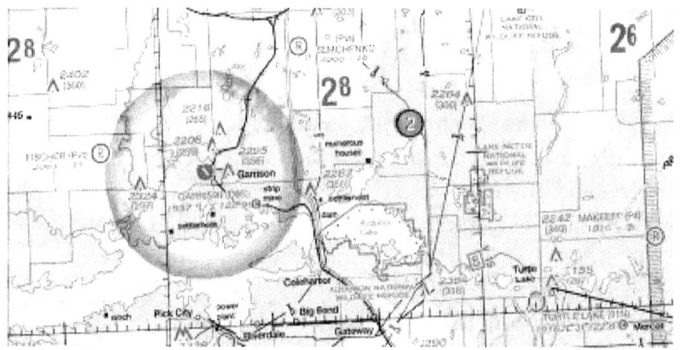

6. You have been hired by a farmer to use your small UA to inspect his crops. The area that you are to survey is in the Devil's Lake West MOA, east of area 2. How would you find out if the MOA is active?
A) Refer to the legend for special use airspace phone number.
B) This information is available in the Small UAS database.
C) Refer to the Military Operations Directory.

7. How would a remote PIC "Check NOTAMS" as noted in the CAUTION box regarding the unmarked balloon?
A) By utilizing the B4UFLY mobile application.
B) By contacting the FAA district office.

C) By obtaining a briefing via an online source such as: 1800WXBrief.com.

8. To ensure that the unmanned aircraft center of gravity (CG) limits are not exceeded, follow the aircraft loading instructions specified in the
A) Pilot's Operating Handbook of UAS Flight Manual
B) Aeronautical Information Manual (AIM)
C) Aircraft Weight and Balance Handbook

9. When operating an unmanned airplane, the remote pilot should consider that the load factor on the wings may be increased any time
A) the CG is shifted rearward to the aft CG limit.
B) the airplane is subjected to maneuvers other than straight-and-level-flight.
C) the gross weight is reduced.

10. A stall occurs when the smooth airflow over the unmanned airplane's wing is disrupted and the lift degenerates rapidly. This is caused when the wing
A) exceeds the maximum speed.
B) exceeds maximum allowable operating weight.
C) exceeds its critical angle of attack.

SAMPLE SUA EXAM

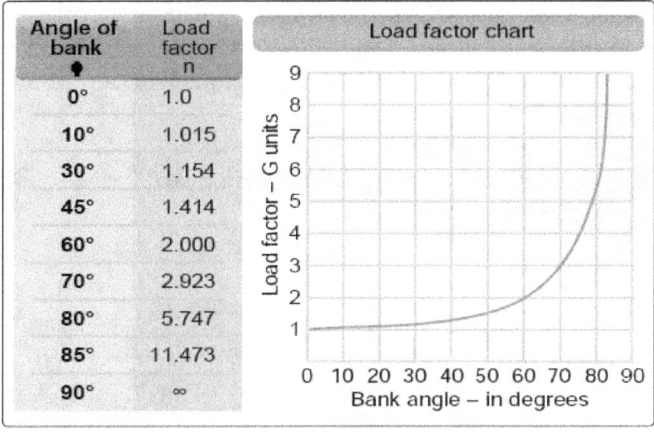

Figure 2.—Load Factor Chart.

11. If an unmanned airplane weighs 33 pounds, what approximate weight would the airplane's structure be required to support during a 30 degree banked turn while maintaining altitude?
A) 34 pounds
B) 47 pounds
C) 38 pounds

12. Which is true regarding the presence of alcohol within the human body?
A) A small amount of alcohol increases vision acuity.
B) Consuming an equal amount of water will increase the destruction of alcohol and alleviate a hangover.
C) Judgment and decision-making abilities can be adversely affected by even small amounts of alcohol.

13. When using a small UA in a commercial operation, who is responsible for briefing the participants about the procedures?
A) The FAA inspector-in-charge.
B) The lead visual observer.
C) The remote PIC.

14. To avoid a possible collision with a manned airplane, you estimate that your small UA climbed to an altitude greater than 600 feet AGL. To whom must you report the deviation?
A) Air Traffic Control
B) The National Transportation Safety Board.
C) Upon request of the FAA.

Figure 26

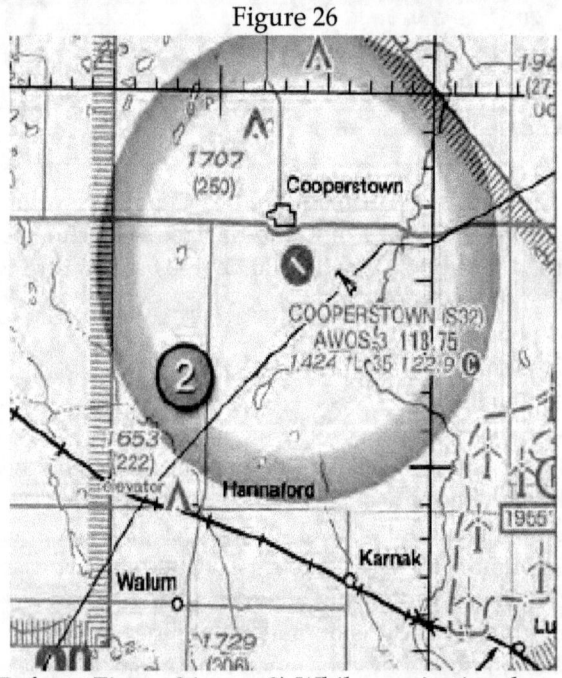

15. (Refer to Figure 26, area 2) While monitoring the Cooperstown CTAF you hear an aircraft announce that they are midfield left downwind to RWY 13. Where would the aircraft be relative to the runway?
A) The aircraft is East.
B) The aircraft is South.
C) The aircraft is West.

16. Under what condition should the operator of a small UA establish scheduled maintenance protocol?
A) When the manufacturer does not provide a maintenance schedule.
B) UAS does not need a required maintenance schedule.
C) When the FAA requires you to, following an accident.

17. According to 14 CFR Part 107, the responsibility to inspect the small UAS to ensure it is in a safe operating condition rests with the
A) remote pilot-in-command.
B) visual observer.
C) owner of the small UAS.

18. Identify the hazardous attitude or characteristic a remote pilot displays while taking risks in order to impress others.
A) Impulsivity.
B) Invulnerability.
C) Macho.

19. You are a remote pilot for a co-op energy service provider. You are to use your UA to inspect power lines in a remote area 15 hours away from your home office. After you drive, the fatigue impacts your abilities to complete your assignment on time. Fatigue can be recognized
A) easily by an experienced pilot.
B) as being in an impaired state.
C) by an ability to overcome sleep deprivation.

20. Safety is an important element for a remote pilot to consider prior to operating an unmanned aircraft system. To prevent the final "link" in the accident chain, a remote pilot must consider which methodology?
A) Crew Resource Management.
B) Safety Management System.

C) Risk Management

21. When adapting crew resource management (CRM) concepts to the operation of a small UA, CRM must be integrated into
A) the flight portion only.
B) all phases of the operation.
C) the communications only.

22. You have been hired as a remote pilot by a local TV news station to film breaking news with a small UA. You expressed safety concerns and the station manager has instructed you to "fly first, ask questions later." What type of hazardous attitude does the attitude represent?
A) Machismo
B) Invulnerability
C) Impulsivity

23. A local TV station has hired a remote pilot to operate their small UA to cover news stories. The remote pilot has had multiple near misses with obstacles on the ground and two small UAS accidents. What would be a solution for the new station to improve their operating safety culture?
A) The news station should implement a policy of no more than five crashes/incidents in 6 months.
B) The news station does not need to make any changes; there are times that an accident is unavoidable.
C) The news station should recognize hazardous attitudes and situations and develop standard operating procedures that emphasize safety.

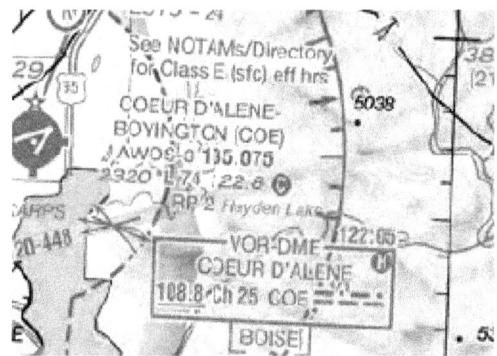

24. At Coeur D'Alene which frequency should be used as a Common Traffic Advisory Frequency (CTAF) to monitor airport traffic?
A) 122.05 MHz
B) 135.075 MHz
C) 122.8 MHz

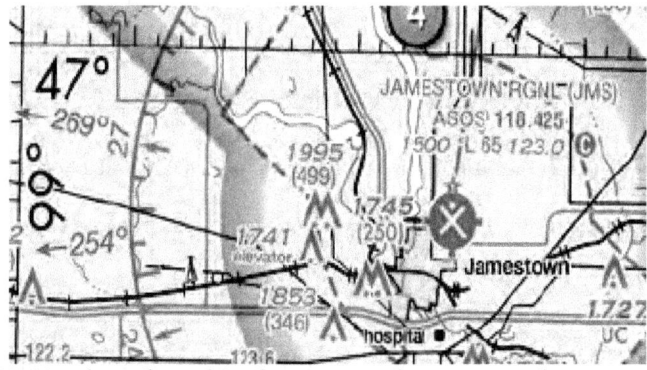

25. You have been hired to inspect the tower under construction at 46.9N and 98.6 W, near Jamestown Regional (JMS). What must you receive prior to flying your unmanned aircraft in this area?
A) Authorization from the military.
B) Authorization from ATC.
C) Authorization from the National Park Service.

26. With ATC authorization, you are operating your small unmanned aircraft approximately 4 SM southeast of Elizabeth City Regional Airport (ECG). What hazard is indicated to be in that area?
A) High density military operations in the vicinity.
B) Unmarked balloon on a cable up to 3,008 AGL.
C) Unmarked balloon on a cable up to 3,008 MSL.

27. The most comprehensive information on a given airport is provided by
A) the Chart Supplements U.S. (formerly Airport Facility Directory).
B) Notices to Airmen (NOTAMS).
C) Terminal Area Chart (TAC).

28. According to 14 CFR Part 107, who is responsible for determining the performance of a small unmanned aircraft?
A) Remote pilot-in-command.
B) Manufacturer.
C) Owner or operator.

29. Which technique should a remote pilot use to scan for traffic? A remote pilot should

A) systematically focus on different segments of the sky for short intervals.
B) concentrate on relative movement detected in the peripheral vision area.
C) continuously scan the sky from right to left.

30. Under what condition would a small UA not have to be registered before it is operated in the United States?
A) When the aircraft weighs less than .55 pounds on takeoff, including everything that is on-board or attached to the aircraft.
B) When the aircraft has a takeoff weight that is more than .55 pounds, but less than 55 pounds, not including fuel and necessary attachments.
C) All small UAS need to be registered regardless of the weight of the aircraft before, during or after the flight.

31. According to 14 CFR Part 48, when must a person register a small UA with the FAA?
A) All civilian small UAS weighing greater than .55 pounds must be registered regardless of its intended use.
B) When the small UA is used for any purpose other than as a model aircraft.
C) Only when the operator will be paid for commercial services.

32. According to 14 CFR Part 48, when would a small UA owner not be permitted to register it?
A) If the owner is less than 13 years of age.
B) All persons must register their small UA.
C) If the owner does not have a valid United States driver's license.

33. According to 14 CFR Part 107, how may a remote pilot operate an unmanned aircraft in Class C airspace?
A) The remote pilot must have prior authorization from

the Air Traffic Control (ATC) having jurisdiction over that airspace.
B) The remote pilot must monitor the ATC frequency from launch to recovery.
C) The remote pilot must contact the ATC facility after launching the unmanned aircraft.

34. According to 14 CFR Part 107, what is required to operate a small UA within 30 minutes after official sunset?
A) Use of anti-collision lights.
B) Must be operated in a rural area.
C) Use of a transponder.

35. You have received an outlook briefing from flight service through 1800WXBrief.com. The briefing indicates you can expect a low-level temperature inversion with high relative humidity. What weather conditions would you expect?
A) Smooth air, poor visibility, fog, haze, or low clouds.
B) Light wind shear, poor visibility, haze and light rain.
C) Turbulent air, poor visibility, fog, low stratus type clouds and showery precipitation.

36. What effect does high density altitude have on the efficiency of a UA propeller?
A) Propeller efficiency is increased.
B) Propeller efficiency is decreased.
C) Density altitude does not affect propeller efficiency.

37. What are characteristics of a moist, unstable air mass?
A) Turbulence and showery precipitation.
B) Poor visibility and smooth air.
C) Haze and smoke.

38. What are the characteristics of stable air?
A) Good visibility and steady precipitation.
B) Poor visibility and steady precipitation.
C) Poor visibility and intermittent precipitation.

Figure 12

```
METAR KINK 121845Z 11012G18KT 15SM SKC 25/17 A3000

METAR KBOI 121854Z 13004KT 30SM SCT150 17/6 A3015

METAR KLAX 121852Z 25004KT 6SM BR SCT007 SCT250 16/15 A2991

SPECI KMDW 121856Z 32005KT 1 1/2SM RA OVC007 17/16 A2980 RMK RAB35

SPECI KJFK 121853Z 18004KT 1/2SM FG R04/2200 OVC005 20/18 A3006
```

39. (Refer to Figure 12) The wind direction and velocity at KJFK is from
A) 180 degrees true at 4 knots.
B) 180 degrees magnetic at 4 knots.
C) 040 degrees true at 18 knots.

40. (Refer to Figure 12) What are the current conditions for Chicago Midway Airport (KMDW)?
A) Sky 700 feet overcast, visibility 1-1/2 SM, rain.
B) Sky 7,000 feet overcast, visibility 1-1/2 SM, heavy rain.
C) Sky 700 feet overcast, visibility 11, occasionally 2 SM, with rain.

Sample UAS Exam ANSWERS

1. What airport is located at approximately 47 degrees, 40 minutes N latitude and 101 degrees, 26 minutes W longitude?
A) Mercer County Regional Airport
B) Semshenko Airport
C) Garrison Airport

> You can count each degree and minute, by looking at the tick marks. Look at the chart, find 47 degree North, (by finding 48 and looking south) and go up, (because it is more than 47) a little bit (the tick marks look like they are in fives). Same with 101 degrees W longitude. Just go a little west (left) of the 101 line and count 26 tick marks. There is only one airport anywhere near here, Garrison. C.

2. What does the line of latitude at area 4 measure?
A) The degrees of latitude east and west of the Prime Meridian.
B) The degrees of latitude north and south of the equator.
C) The degrees of latitude east and west of the line that passes through Greenwich, England.

You do not have to look at the chart to answer this correctly. Lines of latitude measure North and South, like a ladder. Both answers A and C define longitude, east and west. There is only one North/South answer. B.

3. What is the floor of the Savannah Class C airspace at the shelf area (outer circle)?
A) 1,300 feet AGL
B) 1,300 feet MSL
C) 1,700 feet MSL

The chart shows a "13" on the bottom of the fraction for "floor". You know you must add two zeros to make it 1,300. Nobody flying cares about AGL, because everything in an aircraft is measured from Sea Level, a constant. B.

4. The chart shows a gray line with "VR1667, VR1617, VR1638 and VR1668." Could this area present a hazard to the operations of small UA?
A) No, all operations will be above 400 feet.
B) Yes, this is a Military Training Route from the surface to 1,500 AGL.
C) Yes, the defined route provides traffic separation to manned aircraft.

The big clue here is "could". Yeah, almost anything "could" cause a hazard. You should know that the lines are for Military Training Routes, and because they all contain 4 numbers, no segments will be above 1,500 MSL. These planes are flying low and they are flying fast! That's what an MTR is, a freeway for military aircraft to fly fast and low. B.

5. According to 14 CFR Part 107, the remote pilot in command (PIC) of a small unmanned aircraft planning to operate within Class C airspace
A) must use a visual observer.
B) is required to file a flight plan.
C) is required to receive ATC authorization.

What is Class C airspace? Controlled airspace. Who controls it? ATC. Who you gonna ask? ATC. C.

6. You have been hired by a farmer to use your small UA to inspect his crops. The area that you are to survey is in the Devil's Lake West MOA, east of area 2. How would you find out if the MOA is active?

A) Refer to the legend for special use airspace phone number.
B) This information is available in the Small UAS database.
C) Refer to the Military Operations Directory.

Don't be fooled by fancy names you never heard of. What is a small UAS database or Military Operations Directory? I have no idea. The legend on a chart can teach you everything you need to know about the chart. C.

7. How would a remote PIC "Check NOTAMS" as noted in the CAUTION box regarding the unmarked balloon?
A) By utilizing the B4UFLY mobile application.
B) By contacting the FAA district office.
C) By obtaining a briefing via an online source such as: 1800WXBrief.com.

How do you check NOTAMS? Do you contact the FAA every time you want to fly? No. Can you get NOTAMS on a weather page? No. What do you need to do before you fly? Check B4UFLY. A.

8. To ensure that the unmanned aircraft center of gravity (CG) limits are not exceeded, follow the aircraft loading instructions specified in the
A) Pilot's Operating Handbook of UAS Flight Manual
B) Aeronautical Information Manual (AIM)
C) Aircraft Weight and Balance Handbook

Who knows what the CG limits are for YOUR particular aircraft, on this particular mission? There is only one way, it must be calculated. That means it cannot be the AIM or a generic handbook. I have never heard of the "Pilot's Operating Handbook of UAS Flight Manual", but I do know the Aircraft Weight and Balance Handbook teaches everything there is to know about loading and how to calculate weight and balance. C.

9. When operating an unmanned airplane, the remote pilot should consider that the load factor on the wings may be increased any time
A) the CG is shifted rearward to the aft CG limit.
B) the airplane is subjected to maneuvers other than straight-and-level-flight.
C) the gross weight is reduced.

We do not have enough information to determine if shifting the weight rearward has any effect on the wing load factor and reducing the weight always reduces the load. Any banked turn, according to the graph, places strain or "G's" on the airframe and wings. B.

10. A stall occurs when the smooth airflow over the unmanned airplane's wing is disrupted and the lift degenerates rapidly. This is caused when the wing
A) exceeds the maximum speed.
B) exceeds maximum allowable operating weight.
C) exceeds its critical angle of attack.

Several things can cause an aircraft to stall, but we are only concerned with the disruption of smooth airflow over the wing. Increasing the speed just generates more lift and adding weight might cause a stall, but it would be because of power limitations, not disrupted airflow. Increasing the angle-of-attack causes a stall by disrupting the smooth airflow. C.

11. If an unmanned airplane weighs 33 pounds, what approximate weight would the airplane's structure be required to support during a 30 degree banked turn while maintaining altitude?
A) 34 pounds

B) 47 pounds
C) 38 pounds

This one takes a little math. Using the numbers (not the graph), what is the load factor for a 30 degree banked turn? 1.154 Simply multiply 1.154 times the weight, 33 pounds, and you get exactly 38 pounds. If you do not have a calculator, break it down into two problems. 1 x 33 pounds (33) plus .154 x 33 pounds (5.082 pounds). These two numbers (33 + 5) added together equal 38. C.

12. Which is true regarding the presence of alcohol within the human body?
A) A small amount of alcohol increases vision acuity.
B) Consuming an equal amount of water will increase the destruction of alcohol and alleviate a hangover.
C) Judgment and decision-making abilities can be adversely affected by even small amounts of alcohol.

This is a free question because you should already know the answer. Alcohol doesn't make things look clearer, that's why we call them "beer goggles". You can drink anything you want, but only time will cure a hangover and remove the alcohol from your system. Drinking water might help with your dehydration...Any amount of alcohol, no matter how small, can adversely affect perception. C.

13. When using a small UA in a commercial operation, who is responsible for briefing the participants about the procedures?
A) The FAA inspector-in-charge.
B) The lead visual observer.
C) The remote PIC.

Who is responsible for ALL aspects of the sUA

SAMPLE SUA EXAM ANSWERS

operation????? C.

14. To avoid a possible collision with a manned airplane, you estimate that your small UA climbed to an altitude greater than 600 feet AGL. To whom must you report the deviation?
A) Air Traffic Control
B) The National Transportation Safety Board.
C) Upon request of the Federal Aviation Administration.

No one was hurt and no damage. This was a Part 107 deviation, not an accident. This only needs to be reported when asked by the FAA. C.

15. While monitoring the Cooperstown CTAF you hear an aircraft announce that they are midfield left downwind to RWY 13. Where would the aircraft be relative to the runway?
A) The aircraft is East.
B) The aircraft is South.
C) The aircraft is West.

Midfield tells us the pilot is East or West of the airstrip, which is oriented to 130 degrees. The pilot is making a left-hand race track turn and is in the "down wind" leg of the turn, which means the wind is at his back and he is heading approximately 310 (130 + 180). This puts him on the east side of the airport. A.

16. Under what condition should the operator of a small UA establish scheduled maintenance protocol?
A) When the manufacturer does not provide a maintenance schedule.
B) UAS does not need a required maintenance schedule.
C) When the FAA requires you to, following an accident.

B is wrong! C is too late! Must be A.

17. According to 14 CFR Part 107, the responsibility to inspect the small UAS to ensure it is in a safe operating condition rests with the
A) remote pilot-in-command.
B) visual observer.
C) owner of the small UAS.

Who is responsible for ALL aspects of the sUA operation???? A.

18. Identify the hazardous attitude or characteristic a remote pilot displays while taking risks in order to impress others.
A) Impulsivity.
B) Invulnerability.
C) Macho.

"Hey everyone, watch this!" Macho. C.

19. You are a remote pilot for a co-op energy service provider. You are to use your UA to inspect power lines in a remote area 15 hours away from your home office. After you drive, the fatigue impacts your abilities to complete your assignment on time. Fatigue can be recognized
A) easily by an experienced pilot.
B) as being in an impaired state.
C) by an ability to overcome sleep deprivation.

20. This one is tricky. A sounds OK-ish, but B is a better answer. C is just crazy talk. B.

Safety is an important element for a remote pilot to consider prior to operating an unmanned aircraft system. To prevent the final "link" in the accident chain, a remote

pilot must consider which methodology?
A) Crew Resource Management.
B) Safety Management System.
C) Risk Management

Human error is the number one cause of accidents. This comes from a failure to properly manage risk. C.

21. When adapting crew resource management (CRM) concepts to the operation of a small UA, CRM must be integrated into
A) the flight portion only.
B) all phases of the operation.
C) the communications only.

CRM covers aircraft and crew and should be included in all phases of the operation. B.

22. You have been hired as a remote pilot by a local TV news station to film breaking news with a small UA. You expressed safety concerns and the station manager has instructed you to "fly first, ask questions later." What type of hazardous attitude does the attitude represent?
A) Machismo
B) Invulnerability
C) Impulsivity

This one is tricky. Macho is wrong, because you are not calling attention to yourself. Invulnerability sounds like "nothing can happen to me". Impulsivity is the only answer that has "time" as a factor. Hurry up and do it! C.

23. A local TV station has hired a remote pilot to operate their small UA to cover news stories. The remote pilot has had multiple near misses with obstacles on the ground and two small UAS accidents. What would be a solution

SO YOU WANNA BE A DRONE PILOT?

for the new station to improve their operating safety culture?
A) The news station should implement a policy of no more than five crashes/incidents in 6 months.
B) The news station does not need to make any changes; there are times that an accident is unavoidable.
C) The news station should recognize hazardous attitudes and situations and develop standard operating procedures that emphasize safety.

They key words in the question are "solution improve safety culture." One crash is too many, A is wrong. The question asks us to find a solution, not blow off the problem. Standard operating procedures emphasizing safety sounds good. C.

24. At Coeur D'Alene which frequency should be used as a Common Traffic Advisory Frequency (CTAF) to monitor airport traffic?
A) 122.05 MHz
B) 135.075 MHz
C) 122.8 MHz

The C in the circle next to 122.8 shows this is the CTAF frequency. C.

25. You have been hired to inspect the tower under construction at 46.9N and 98.6 W, near Jamestown Regional (JMS). What must you receive prior to flying your unmanned aircraft in this area?
A) Authorization from the military.
B) Authorization from ATC.
C) Authorization from the National Park Service.

Don't look for a tower, because it is under construction and not shown! I don't see any military or National Parks

SAMPLE SUA EXAM ANSWERS

nearby. I do see flight paths from the airport. B.

26. With ATC authorization, you are operating your small unmanned aircraft approximately 4 SM southeast of Elizabeth City Regional Airport (ECG). What hazard is indicated to be in that area?
A) High density military operations in the vicinity.
B) Unmarked balloon on a cable up to 3,008 AGL.
C) Unmarked balloon on a cable up to 3,008 MSL.

There is a warning box noting the balloon at 3,008 MSL. C.

27. The most comprehensive information on a given airport is provided by
A) the Chart Supplements U.S. (formerly Airport Facility Directory).
B) Notices to Airmen (NOTAMS).
C) Terminal Area Chart (TAC).

NOTAMS tell you where you can't fly and TAC charts give airport data, but not as much as the Chart Supplement. A.

28. According to 14 CFR Part 107, who is responsible for determining the performance of a small unmanned aircraft?
A) Remote pilot-in-command.
B) Manufacturer.
C) Owner or operator.

Who is responsible for ALL sUA operations?????? A.

29. Which technique should a remote pilot use to scan for traffic? A remote pilot should
A) systematically focus on different segments of the sky for short intervals.

B) concentrate on relative movement detected in the peripheral vision area.
C) continuously scan the sky from right to left.

"A" wants you to focus and "B" wants you to concentrate, neither of which is scanning. "C" even has the word "scan" in it! C.

30. Under what condition would a small UA not have to be registered before it is operated in the United States?
A) When the aircraft weighs less than .55 pounds on takeoff, including everything that is on-board or attached to the aircraft.
B) When the aircraft has a takeoff weight that is more than .55 pounds, but less than 55 pounds, not including fuel and necessary attachments.
C) All small UAS need to be registered regardless of the weight of the aircraft before, during or after the flight.

This is from the fine print on registration. Under .55 pounds at lift off does not need to be registered. A.

31. According to 14 CFR Part 48, when must a person register a small UA with the FAA?
A) All civilian small UA weighing greater than .55 pounds must be registered regardless of its intended use.
B) When the small UA is used for any purpose other than as a model aircraft.
C) Only when the operator will be paid for commercial services.

Over .55 pounds must be registered, regardless of why you are flying. Hobbyists register the person, RPICs register each aircraft, but you must be registered! A.

SAMPLE SUA EXAM ANSWERS

32. According to 14 CFR Part 48, when would a small UA owner not be permitted to register it?
A) If the owner is less than 13 years of age.
B) All persons must register their small UA.
C) If the owner does not have a valid United States driver's license.

You must be 13 years of age or older if you are a human (corporations can be any age) to register an aircraft. Most 13-year olds do not have a driver's license. You are still too young to be an RPIC (age 16), but you can fly for hobby or under the supervision of an RPIC. A.

33. According to 14 CFR Part 107, how may a remote pilot operate an unmanned aircraft in Class C airspace?
A) The remote pilot must have prior authorization from the Air Traffic Control (ATC) having jurisdiction over that airspace.
B) The remote pilot must monitor the ATC frequency from launch to recovery.
C) The remote pilot must contact the ATC facility after launching the unmanned aircraft.

No one flies in controlled airspace without permission from who? ATC. Why should you be different? "B" is not wrong, but it is not the correct answer. "C" is wrong. A.

34. According to 14 CFR Part 107, what is required to operate a small UA within 30 minutes after official sunset?
A) Use of anti-collision lights.
B) Must be operated in a rural area.
C) Use of a transponder.

You can fly at dusk and dawn if you have anti-collision lights visible three miles. Dusk is up to 30 minutes after sunset. A.

SO YOU WANNA BE A DRONE PILOT?

35. You have received an outlook briefing from flight service through 1800WXBrief.com. The briefing indicates you can expect a low-level temperature inversion with high relative humidity. What weather conditions would you expect?
A) Smooth air, poor visibility, fog, haze, or low clouds.
B) Light wind shear, poor visibility, haze and light rain.
C) Turbulent air, poor visibility, fog, low stratus type clouds and showery precipitation.

Wind shear is violent, turbulent air is violent, low-level temperature inversion is calm. A.

36. What effect does high density altitude have on the efficiency of a UA propeller?
A) Propeller efficiency is increased.
B) Propeller efficiency is decreased.
C) Density altitude does not affect propeller efficiency.

Thin air, up high, doesn't work as good. B.

37. What are characteristics of a moist, unstable air mass?
A) Turbulence and showery precipitation.
B) Poor visibility and smooth air.
C) Haze and smoke.

Smooth air and haze are calm. Turbulence is unstable. A.

38. What are the characteristics of stable air?
A) Good visibility and steady precipitation.
B) Poor visibility and steady precipitation.
C) Poor visibility and intermittent precipitation.

Good visibility isn't stable air. Intermittent rain isn't stable. B.

SAMPLE SUA EXAM ANSWERS

39. The wind direction and velocity at KJFK is from
A) 180 degrees true at 4 knots.
B) 180 degrees magnetic at 4 knots.
C) 040 degrees true at 18 knots.

You don't have to look at the chart. Remember how wind is noted? Three digit direction, two digit speed and "KT" for knots. How is wind measured? Degrees magnetic, because no one knows where true North is and the compass shows magnetic North. B.

40. What are the current conditions for Chicago Midway Airport (KMDW)?
A) Sky 700 feet overcast, visibility 1-1/2 SM, rain.
B) Sky 7,000 feet overcast, visibility 1-1/2 SM, heavy rain.
C) Sky 700 feet overcast, visibility 11, occasionally 2 SM, with rain.

OVC 007 shows overcast at 700 feet and visibility at 1 ½ SM. A.